服务外包工程教育规划教材

全国服务外包人才培养高峰论坛组织编写

软件外包
行业英语读写教程

张冬瑜 李映夏 主编
杜宛宜 周纯岳 樊宇 于红 副主编

清华大学出版社
北京

内 容 简 介

近年来,我国软件外包行业取得了蓬勃发展,对既懂英语又懂技术的高层次复合型人才有更加迫切的需求。培养大批具有较强英语理解和沟通能力的从业者是加快软件外包行业与国际接轨进程的重要条件。《软件外包行业英语读写教程》一书将帮助计算机软件相关专业的学生及IT从业者熟悉和掌握更多的专业英语词汇与表达,提高软件外包行业的英语阅读水平与在实际工作中的写作技能。

本教材呈现了软件外包行业的完整流程,涉及外包各个工作环节的信息。每个单元的主题介绍部分用精练的语言介绍与阅读主题相关的背景知识,让读者对这一单元的主题有一个整体把握。阅读内容专业性强,同时力求内容活泼有趣和练习的形式多样。每单元后都附有英汉对照词汇表,便于读者自学。详细的写作技巧的介绍为读者打好写作基础,具体的写作实例提供了真实的写作样本。案例分析的选材强调真实性,案例与单元主题紧密相关。通过真实工作情境中阅读材料的语言输入,达到提高读者语言水平和用英语作为工作语言进行交流的目的。教材采用专业教师+英语教师+IT行业人员三合一的开发模式,集中了软件外包行业知识的基础和精华。专业人士给予教材精准的知识定位,英语教师设计了语言学习任务,充分发挥各方专长。教材在编写过程中进行了广泛调研,并参考借鉴相关的行业标准。

本书既可以作为高等院校培养学生以英语为媒介来了解软件外包行业基础知识的阅读课或选修课教材,也适用于具有一定英语水平的社会人员及对软件外包领域感兴趣的从业人员;既可以用于课堂教学,也可以用于自学。

本书封面贴有清华大学出版社防伪标签,无标签者不得销售。
版权所有,侵权必究。侵权举报电话:010-62782989 13701121933

图书在版编目(CIP)数据

软件外包行业英语读写教程/张冬瑜,李映夏主编. --北京:清华大学出版社,2015(2020.2重印)
服务外包工程教育规划教材
ISBN 978-7-302-38254-6

Ⅰ.①软… Ⅱ.①张… ②李… Ⅲ.①软件-对外承包-英语-阅读教学-教材 ②软件-对外承包-英语-写作-教材 Ⅳ.①H31

中国版本图书馆CIP数据核字(2014)第235237号

责任编辑:白立军　薛　阳
封面设计:常雪影
责任校对:李建庄
责任印制:宋　林

出版发行:清华大学出版社
　　　　网　　址:http://www.tup.com.cn, http://www.wqbook.com
　　　　地　　址:北京清华大学学研大厦A座　　　邮　编:100084
　　　　社 总 机:010-62770175　　　　　　　　　邮　购:010-62786544
　　　　投稿与读者服务:010-62776969, c-service@tup.tsinghua.edu.cn
　　　　质量反馈:010-62772015, zhiliang@tup.tsinghua.edu.cn
　　　　课件下载:http://www.tup.com.cn, 010-83470236

印 装 者:北京虎彩文化传播有限公司
经　　销:全国新华书店
开　　本:185mm×260mm　　　印　张:8.75　　　字　数:215千字
版　　次:2015年2月第1版　　　　　　　　　　　印　次:2020年2月第4次印刷
定　　价:22.00元

产品编号:059237-01

服务外包工程教育规划教材
编写委员会

主任：
何积丰　中国科学院院士

执行主任：
詹国华　杭州师范大学杭州国际服务工程学院执行院长

副主任（按拼音排序）：
鲍　泓　北京联合大学副校长
顾　明　国家服务外包人力资源研究院、清华大学软件学院副院长
罗军舟　东南大学计算机学院、软件学院院长
温　涛　大连东软信息学院院长
杨小虎　浙江大学软件学院副院长、浙大网新副总裁
常晋义　常熟理工学院国际服务工程学院院长
吴克寿　厦门理工学院软件与服务外包学院院长

委员（按拼音排序）：

白　云	包　健	常中华	陈　刚	陈超祥	陈春玲	陈永强	樊光辉
樊丽淑	冯秀君	宫冠英	顾玲妹	顾永根	郭　权	何世明	胡俊云
黄　斌	蒋晓舰	黎　明	李　兢	李继芳	李黎青	李占军	李正帆
凌　云	刘　清	刘国龙	刘海麓	刘锦高	刘俊成	刘勇兵	刘正涛
卢　雷	卢维亮	陆　冰	马长伟	毛爱亮	倪筱斌	秦绪好	屈中华
邵　云	邵定宏	沈　洪	沈荣大	施永进	石　冰	石　峰	宋旭明
孙崇理	孙建国	汤　伟	田详宏	屠立忠	万　健	王　军	王　瑞
王斌耀	王秉全	王汉成	王红娅	王杰华	王青青	王万良	吴鸿雁
吴育锋	徐瑞兰	徐文彬	徐一旻	宣舒钧	宣逸芬	薛锦云	严盈富
杨　方	杨东勇	杨欢聋	杨季文	杨起帆	叶　林	叶时平	叶勇抱
易　勇	应　晶	余　军	余国扬	袁　玫	袁兆山	袁贞明	张　民
张瑞林	张少华	张慰兮	张玉华	张再越	赵　辉	赵　梅	郑　涛
郑志军	支芬和	周　宇	朱春风	朱彦蓉	祝建中		

策划编辑：
袁勤勇　清华大学出版社

1. 编写宗旨

随着我国高等教育的不断发展,仅仅能够熟练掌握英语语言知识和技能已经无法满足大学语言教育的要求了。把学生培养成为懂专业,并且使用英语进行专业知识交流的复合型人才,才能使培养出的人才更好地与社会接轨。ESP(特殊用途英语)的出现成为顺应了这一大趋势的必然。近十年来,软件行业在中国得到迅猛发展。软件行业对于人才的需求在数量,更重要的是质量方面,不断提高。面临这样的机遇和挑战,培养大批优秀的软件产业的人才成为全国各高校的紧迫任务。

从 2001 年开始,教育部和发展计划委员会先后批准在全国重点高校中建立了 37 所国家示范性软件学院。软件外包行业的国际化属性决定了这一行业的人才应具备使用外语进行工作交流、文件信息处理及实际操作问题的解决。然而,处在教学一线的教师和科研工作者发现,大学的英语教材基本都是以语言交际训练为主要编写内容的,涉及软件外包专业知识的英语教材几乎为空白。为了弥补这一缺失,本书作者结合国际先进的教学理念,结合多年积累的教学实践,倾力编写本教材。《软件外包行业英语读写教程》以阅读为基础,扩大学生的英语词汇和表达;同时,培养学生独立思考的能力,让学生更好地用英语讨论和解决实际工作中出现的问题。对于 IT 从业者,本书为提高其英语水平和实际工作交往的沟通协调能力提供了很好的帮助。

2. 教材结构

本书由 9 个单元组成,模拟了软件外包行业的完整流程,涉及外包简介、软件外包企业文化、客户服务、工作交流、常见的开发模式和行业标准、设计过程、编码过程、测试过程、有效性验证、质量控制、解决问题及外包项目的收尾工作等方面的信息。每个单元一个主题,由四大部分组成。

第一部分为深度阅读课文,由一篇与主题内容相关的文章构成。围绕这一篇主题阅读又分为:

① 主题介绍——用精练的语言介绍与阅读主题相关的背景知识，让读者对这一单元的主题有一个整体把握；

② 阅读前的热身问题——激发读者的学习兴趣；

③ 词汇表——重点列出行业术语，英汉对照词汇表，便于读者自学；词汇练习——包括词汇定义匹配题，课文词汇填空题，课文句子翻译等，帮助读者进一步掌握新词；

④ 课文理解——包括根据课文内容判断对错，回答问题等几部分。

第二部分为延伸阅读——重点拓展读者视野，在主题阅读的基础上加深对这一主题的理解，并配有相应练习，形式多样，注重实用性。

第三部分的写作部分依托英语的工作语言环境，强调实用性的写作技能指导和训练。详细的写作技巧的介绍为读者打好写作基础，具体的写作实例提供了真实的写作样本。

第四部分是案例分析。选材强调真实性，案例与单元主题紧密相关。单元主题设计环环相扣，完整地呈现了软件外包的整个环节。通过真实工作情境中阅读材料的语言输入，达到提高读者语言水平和用英语作为工作语言进行交流的目的。

3. 编写队伍

《软件外包行业英语读写教程》编写组包括以下成员：苏华玲、崔紫娟。他们在保持日常教学、培训与科研工作的同时，严格认真、按质按量地完成了本教程的编写工作；他们以高度的责任心和丰富的专业知识对文稿进行了多次校对与润色，使本书在质量上有了可靠的保障。

由于编者水平有限，疏漏之处在所难免，敬请专家与读者不吝指正，以便再版时更正和改进。

目 录

Unit One　Knowing Outsourcing Industry ………………………………… 1

  Part One　　Reading ………………………………………………………… 1
  Part Two　　Writing ………………………………………………………… 10
  Part Three　 Case Study …………………………………………………… 11

Unit Two　Managing Culture in Outsourcing ……………………………… 14

  Part One　　Reading ………………………………………………………… 14
  Part Two　　Writing ………………………………………………………… 21
  Part Three　 Case Study …………………………………………………… 25

Unit Three　Handling Clients ………………………………………………… 28

  Part One　　Reading ………………………………………………………… 28
  Part Two　　Writing ………………………………………………………… 37
  Part Three　 Case Study …………………………………………………… 39

Unit Four　Working Together ………………………………………………… 42

  Part One　　Reading ………………………………………………………… 42
  Part Two　　Writing ………………………………………………………… 51
  Part Three　 Case Study …………………………………………………… 54

Unit Five　Initiation …………………………………………………………… 56

  Part One　　Reading ………………………………………………………… 56
  Part Two　　Writing ………………………………………………………… 65
  Part Three　 Case Study …………………………………………………… 69

Unit Six　Design ……………………………………………………………… 72

  Part One　　Reading ………………………………………………………… 72
  Part Two　　Writing ………………………………………………………… 81

    Part Three   Case Study ⋯⋯⋯⋯⋯⋯⋯⋯⋯⋯⋯⋯⋯⋯⋯⋯⋯⋯⋯⋯⋯⋯⋯⋯⋯ 84

Unit Seven   Coding ⋯⋯⋯⋯⋯⋯⋯⋯⋯⋯⋯⋯⋯⋯⋯⋯⋯⋯⋯⋯⋯⋯⋯⋯⋯⋯⋯⋯⋯ 86

    Part One   Reading ⋯⋯⋯⋯⋯⋯⋯⋯⋯⋯⋯⋯⋯⋯⋯⋯⋯⋯⋯⋯⋯⋯⋯⋯⋯⋯⋯ 86
    Part Two   Writing ⋯⋯⋯⋯⋯⋯⋯⋯⋯⋯⋯⋯⋯⋯⋯⋯⋯⋯⋯⋯⋯⋯⋯⋯⋯⋯⋯⋯ 95
    Part Three   Case Study ⋯⋯⋯⋯⋯⋯⋯⋯⋯⋯⋯⋯⋯⋯⋯⋯⋯⋯⋯⋯⋯⋯⋯⋯⋯ 97

Unit Eight   Software Testing ⋯⋯⋯⋯⋯⋯⋯⋯⋯⋯⋯⋯⋯⋯⋯⋯⋯⋯⋯⋯⋯⋯⋯⋯ 100

    Part One   Reading ⋯⋯⋯⋯⋯⋯⋯⋯⋯⋯⋯⋯⋯⋯⋯⋯⋯⋯⋯⋯⋯⋯⋯⋯⋯⋯ 100
    Part Two   Writing ⋯⋯⋯⋯⋯⋯⋯⋯⋯⋯⋯⋯⋯⋯⋯⋯⋯⋯⋯⋯⋯⋯⋯⋯⋯⋯⋯ 108
    Part Three   Case Study ⋯⋯⋯⋯⋯⋯⋯⋯⋯⋯⋯⋯⋯⋯⋯⋯⋯⋯⋯⋯⋯⋯⋯⋯ 112

Unit Nine   Release Management ⋯⋯⋯⋯⋯⋯⋯⋯⋯⋯⋯⋯⋯⋯⋯⋯⋯⋯⋯⋯⋯⋯ 113

    Part One   Reading ⋯⋯⋯⋯⋯⋯⋯⋯⋯⋯⋯⋯⋯⋯⋯⋯⋯⋯⋯⋯⋯⋯⋯⋯⋯⋯ 113
    Part Two   Writing ⋯⋯⋯⋯⋯⋯⋯⋯⋯⋯⋯⋯⋯⋯⋯⋯⋯⋯⋯⋯⋯⋯⋯⋯⋯⋯⋯ 119
    Part Three   Case Study ⋯⋯⋯⋯⋯⋯⋯⋯⋯⋯⋯⋯⋯⋯⋯⋯⋯⋯⋯⋯⋯⋯⋯⋯ 125

References ⋯⋯⋯⋯⋯⋯⋯⋯⋯⋯⋯⋯⋯⋯⋯⋯⋯⋯⋯⋯⋯⋯⋯⋯⋯⋯⋯⋯⋯⋯⋯⋯⋯⋯⋯ 127

Unit One

Knowing Outsourcing Industry

Note on the topic

软件外包就是企业为了专注核心竞争力业务和降低软件项目成本,将软件项目中的全部或部分工作发包给提供外包服务的企业完成的软件需求活动。现在业务流程外包(BPO)已经成为外包服务新的发展趋势,在未来几年内将成为外包的主要内容。BPO 包括人力资源、采购、财会、客户中心、后勤、研发、营销、工厂运作、培训,这些大类还可以进一步细分。不仅 IT 行业需要 BPO,而且 BPO 的每项业务都离不开 IT 业务的支持,从而产生 IT 外包机会。

外包服务怎样才能充分发挥其作用? 外包服务经历哪些阶段? 采用外包服务要注意哪些问题? 这些就是本章将要讨论的问题。

Part One Reading

I. Before you read

A. Discuss the following questions in a group.

1) Which of the following businesses are service industries?
- Advertising.
- Child care.
- Education.
- Financial service.
- Health care.
- Insurance.
- Banking.
- Practice of law.
- Marketing.
- Tourism.
- House building.

2) True or false.
- The service industries involve the provision of services to businesses as

well as final consumers.
- A service Industry is one where no goods are produced whereas primary industries are those that extract minerals, oil etc. from the ground and secondary industries are those that manufacture products, including builders, but not remodeling contractors.

B. *Skim the text and answer the following questions:*
1) What is outsourcing?
2) What are the most common forms of outsourcing?
3) What are the three factors that all outsourcing cases depend on?

II. Text Reading

What is Outsourcing?

Outsourcing is contracting with another company or person to do a particular function. Almost every organization outsources in some way. Typically, the function being outsourced is considered non-core to the business. An insurance company, for example, might outsource its **janitorial** and **landscaping** operations to firms that **specialize** in those types of work since they are not related to insurance or strategic to the business. The outside firms that are providing the outsourcing services are third-party providers, or as they are more commonly called, service providers.

Although outsourcing has been around as long as work specialization has existed, in recent history, companies began employing the outsourcing model to carry out narrow functions, such as **payroll**, **billing** and data entry. Those processes could be done more efficiently and therefore more cost-effectively, by other companies with specialized tools and facilities and specially trained **personnel**.

Currently, outsourcing takes many forms. Organizations still hire service providers to handle **distinct** business processes, such as benefits management. But some organizations outsource whole operations. The most common forms are Information Technology Outsourcing (ITO) and Business Process Outsourcing (BPO). Business Process Outsourcing encompasses call center outsourcing, Human Resources Outsourcing (HRO), finance and accounting outsourcing, and claims processing outsourcing. These outsourcing deals involve multi-year contracts that can run into hundreds of millions of dollars. Frequently, the people performing the work internally for the client firm are transferred and become employees for the service provider.

Some **nimble** companies that are short on time and money, such as start-up software publishers, apply multisourcing—using both internal and service provider staff—in order to speed up the time to launch. They hire a **multitude** of outsourcing service providers to handle almost all aspects of a new project, from product design, to software coding, to testing, to **localization**, and even to marketing and sales.

The process of outsourcing generally **encompasses** four stages: ① strategic thinking, to develop the organization's philosophy about the role of outsourcing in its activities; ② evaluation and selection, to decide on the appropriate outsourcing projects and potential locations for the work to be done and service providers to do it; ③ contract development, to work out the legal, pricing and Service Level Agreement (SLA) terms; and ④ outsourcing management or **governance**, to refine the ongoing working relationship between the client and outsourcing service providers.

In all cases, outsourcing success depends on three factors: executive-level support in the client organization for the outsourcing mission; **ample** communication to affected employees; and the client's ability to manage its service providers. The outsourcing professionals in charge of the work on both the client and provider sides need a combination of skills in such areas as negotiation, communication, project management, the ability to understand the terms and conditions of the contracts and Service Level Agreements (SLAs), and, above all, the willingness to be flexible as business needs change.

The challenges of outsourcing become especially acute when the work is being done in a different country (offshored), since that involves language, cultural and time zone differences.

Outsourcing is a central element of **globalization**, and policymakers need to understand its economic basis if they are to develop effective policy responses. The practice of outsourcing should be understood as a new form of competition and responding to it calls for the development of policies that enhance national competitiveness and establish new rules governing the nature of global competition. Viewing outsourcing through the lens of competition connects with early 20th century American **institutional** economics. The policy challenge is to construct institutions that ensure stable flows of demand and income, **thereby** addressing the Keynesian problem while preserving **incentives** for economic action. This was the approach that was **embedded** in the New Deal, which successfully addressed the problems of the Depression Era. Global outsourcing poses our current economic challenges and its solution requires a new set of institutions. The task is compounded by problems associated with a lack of global **regulatory** institutions and changes in the balance of political power that make it difficult to enact needed reforms.

Global outsourcing is enormously facilitated by technological innovations associated with computing, electronic communication, and the Internet. However, it is important to recognize that the debate surrounding outsourcing is not about the benefits of technology. It is a debate about the nature of competition and who constitutes appropriate rules for governing competition within and between countries. Failure to recognize this can distract and confuse the issue.

(737 words)

Ⅲ. Words to Note

janitorial	a.	保洁部门的
landscaping	n.	景观美化
specialize	v.	专门研究；专攻
payroll	n.	薪水支出
billing	n.	开账单
personnel	n.	职员
distinct	a.	明显的，确切的
nimble	a.	聪明的，机智的
multitude	n.	许多，多数
localization	n.	地方化
encompass	v.	包括
governance	n.	管理
ample	a.	充足的
globalization	n.	全球化
institutional	a.	制度上的
thereby	adj.	因此
incentive	n.	刺激，动力
embed	v.	嵌入
regulatory	a.	管理的，控制的

Ⅳ. Part of Reading section

Read the text and answer the following questions.

1) What is outsourcing?

 _____

2) What is a service provider?

 _____

3) In what way is the recent outsourcing different from the traditional outsourcing?

 _____

4) What are the advantages of outsourcing?

 _____

5) What are the new forms of outsourcing?

 _____

6) What skills do the outsourcing professionals need?

7) What are the acute challenges when the work is being done in another country?

8) What is the debate surrounding global outsourcing about?

V. Vocabulary Building

A. *Match the words with their definitions.*

specialize	a.	exercising authority
distinct	b.	more than enough in size or scope or capacity
nimble	c.	growth to a global or worldwide scale
multitude	d.	a large indefinite number
localization	e.	a determination of the place where something is
encompass	f.	include as a part of something broader
governance	g.	relating to or constituting or involving an institution
ample	h.	a positive motivational influence
globalization	i.	restricting according to rules or principles
institutional	j.	devote oneself to a special area of work
incentive	k.	recognizable; marked
regulatory	l.	mentally quick

B. *Complete sentence with the words given.*

specialize	distinct	multitude	localization	globalization
institutional	incentive	regulatory	ample	encompass

1) Information systems outsourcing companies may _____ in telecommunications, application services, hardware services, desktop services, networking services, administration applications, help desk and many more.

2) Outsourcing contracts generally contain 19 _____ articles that are needed to govern the contract and relationship with the service provider.

3) Still, the complexity of global outsourcing and the _____ of logistics solutions providers courting your business can make the process of finding a partner capable of engaging supply chain stakeholders and customers as an extension of your enterprise a daunting task.

4) In addition to the full outsourcing solution, hybrid alternatives can be used to increase capacity, such as outsourcing more, but not all possible _____ functions.

5) Although outsourcing used to be simply across different companies, it now commonly happens across different countries. This contributes greatly to _____, as the world's economies get more connected and become interdependent, parts of a big web, all relying on each other for success.

6) Investec Asset Management has entered exclusive negotiations with State Street regarding the outsourcing of its _____ administration back office.

7) The _____ and credits written into an IT services contract are critical to the long-term success of an outsourcing deal.

8) Outsourcing in the _____ area may save you money, help your department or company be more flexible and manage the growth of your company effectively. It will also allow your business to gain access to external expertise which you do not have in-house.

9) It is a known fact that India tops the list of world's favorite outsourcing destinations. _____ number of skilled resources, use of latest technology, time zone advantages and cost-effective services are just a few of the reasons for India's popularity.

10) Dimension Data can help you inject more agility and flexibility into your business model by delivering IT outsourcing services that _____ the network, data entry, and many more.

C. Translate the following sentences into Chinese.

1) Outsourcing is contracting with another company or person to do a particular function. Typically, the function being outsourced is considered non-core to the business.

2) An insurance company, for example, might outsource its janitorial and landscaping operations to firms that specialize in those types of work since they are not related to insurance or strategic to the business.

3) Outsourcing is a central element of globalization, and policymakers need to understand its economic basis if they are to develop effective policy responses.

4) The policy challenge is to construct institutions that ensure stable flows of demand and income, thereby addressing the Keynesian problem while preserving incentives for economic action.

D. Read the following passage about the outsourcing stages:

(1) Choose the best heading for each of the paragraphs.

a. Operations Stage

b. Implementation Stage

c. Analysis Stage

(2) Choose the best sentence to fill in each of the blanks in the passage.

a. It has to decide on what level it has to outsource so as to be a profitable organization.

b. One of the biggest questions that arise in the mind of the company is to make or buy the required service or product for the company.

c. The company has to send across managers and consultants to actually implement the business process and design how they actually want the production to go on.

The companies have many processes that have to be integrated while manufacturing, selling, buying, customer sourcing etc. _____ It has to identify analysis and maximize outsourcing opportunities. The stages for outsourcing can be different for different customers but the outsourcing process can be put into three phases:

1. _____

There are various decisions that the company has to make while thinking of outsourcing. _____ The company mostly uses cost benefit analysis with the help of the make or buy model to come to a conclusion whether to buy or make. The analysis stage acts as foundation stone where the company decides if it wants to outsource its function or not.

2. _____

At the operations stage the company will identify and shortlist the service providers and negotiate the terms and conditions with them. The company will undergo this process with various service providers so that they can get the best deal out of the minimum problems.

The company will then select some service providers that the company feels would be the most profitable. The company will negotiate the terms and conditions and keep the format clear on what they are looking for and what is the way the payments would be made, the staff, the operational strategies, raw materials, etc.

3. _____

This stage is the most important and the most difficult stage. _____ The company lays down the framework in place and puts the integration process right. This stage will determine the future flow of the business.

In all cases, outsourcing success depends on three factors: executive-level support in the client organization for the outsourcing mission; ample communication to affected employees; and the client's ability to manage its service providers. The outsourcing professionals in charge of the work on both the client and provider sides need a combination of skills in such areas as negotiation, communication, project management, the ability to understand the terms and conditions of the contracts and service level agreements, and, above all, the willingness to be flexible as business needs change.

VI. Further Reading

Four Global IT Outsourcing Environmental Sustainability Issues

The four environmental sustainability issues that are of key concern to buyers and providers of Global IT Outsourcing (GITO) include power consumption, travel requirements, water supply and electronic waste.

Power. The power consumption of Information and Communication Technologies (ICT) continues to increase with the proliferation of ICT in business. Large IT outsourcing providers consume significant electronic power to operate the ICT infrastructure. Electronic power usually requires the burning of carbon fuels, which in turn produce GreenHouse Gases (GHGs). In addition, the cost of electricity continues to rise as the number of servers and related equipment used increased. As a result, many IT outsourcing providers are taking steps to source greener electricity and to reduce consumption.

Most outsourcing providers are major consumers of electronic power. The increasing power consumptions by information technology infrastructure give rise to two environmental concerns related to IT outsourcing:

(1) The cost of energy impacts IT operations.

(2) Most electricity generation produces GHGs. GHGs have been linked to global warming. It has been estimated that 85% of global energy consumption "is represented by fossil energy, with oil, gas, and coal contributing a roughly equal amounts" and "our energy problem lies in the effects caused by CO_2 produced when fossil fuels are burned".

Travel. The volume of employer travel required for the management of global outsourcing is an environmental concern due to the production of GHGs by aircraft and other means of transportation.

Water. The availability and conservation of fresh water for the large number of employees and communities in outsourcing provider delivery centers is a sustainability concern in India, a major GITO location.

Travel and water consumption is the impacts of humans on the environment. Global IT outsourcing providers have two additional environmental impacts that can be measured: the amount of travel (and related GHG emissions) undertaken by and the amount of fresh water consumption by employees. Air travel is a significant aspect of global outsourcing, especially when developing new business relationships. Researchers at Cranfield University, UK, found that 57% of business people travel for new business relationships, whereas day-to-day management and operations require far less travel. Given the global nature of outsourcing, flying is the predominant mode of travel in the outsourcing business.

Electronic waste. The "e-waste" from end-of-life ICT such as servers, PCs, and communication devices is a significant sustainability issue.

Several jurisdictions have recognized the growing problem of e-waste and have enacted legislation that requires a planned and environmentally appropriate method for disposal of obsolete electronic equipment. In the United States, 19 states have passed legislation mandating e-waste recycling programs. In Canada, the Ontario government has enacted the Waste Diversion Act, which resulted in the industry-led Waste Electrical and Electronic Equipment program (WEEE). This program requires buyers of electronic equipment to pay an upfront disposal fee for equipment such as computers, printers, monitors, etc. The state of California has a consumer electronic waste recycling fee similar to that of the Canadian

program. The European Union has also developed policy and legislation. (504 words)
(Sustainable Global Outsourcing by Ron Babin and Brian Nicolson)

A. Write the full form of the following initials and translate them into Chinese.
1) GITO _____
2) ICT _____
3) GHG _____
4) WEEE _____

B. Summary Writing: Write a summary of 100 words to summarize the passage.

_____
_____
_____
_____
_____
_____
_____

C. Use words you have learnt to explain the underlined words in the sentences below.

1) The power consumption of information and communication technologies (ICT) continues to increase with the <u>proliferation</u> of ICT in business.

2) The increasing power consumptions by information technology infrastructure <u>give rise to</u> two environmental concerns related to IT outsourcing.

3) The cost of energy <u>impacts</u> IT operations.

4) Several jurisdictions have recognized the growing problem of e-waste and have enacted <u>legislation</u> that requires a planned and environmentally appropriate method for disposal of <u>obsolete</u> electronic equipment.

5) This program requires buyers of electronic equipment to pay an <u>upfront</u> disposal fee for equipment such as computers, printers, monitors, etc.

Culture Notes

1) Offshore outsourcing: Offshore outsourcing is the practice of hiring an external organization to perform some business functions in a country other than the one where the products or services are actually developed or manufactured.

2) Keynesian: Keynesian economics is the view that in the short run, especially during recessions, economic output is strongly influenced by aggregate demand (total spending in the economy). In the Keynesian view, aggregate demand does not necessarily equal to the productive capacity of the economy; instead, it is influenced by a host of factors and sometimes behaves erratically, affecting production, employment, and inflation.

3) New Deal: The New Deal was a series of domestic programs enacted in the United States between 1933 and 1938. They involved laws passed by Congress as well as presidential executive orders during the first term of President Franklin D. Roosevelt. The programs were in response to the Great Depression, and focused on what historians call the "3 R's": Relief, Recovery, and Reform. That is Relief for the unemployed and poor; Recovery of the economy to normal levels; and Reform of the financial system to prevent a repeat depression.

Part Two Writing

Writing Skills: Business Writing

As for business writing, everyone needs to write intelligently. By using simple, clear, precise language-and following a few other basic writing rules, you can become a better communicator and improve the prospects for your career.

Clarity is the most important characteristic of good business writing.

Start by using short, declarative sentences. Never use a long word where a short one will do. (No need to write "utilize" when "use" works just as well.) Be ruthless about self-editing; if you don't need a word, cut it.

Never use a foreign phrase, a scientific word, or any kind of jargon if you can think of an English equivalent.

When you're composing a writing, say what you need to say, and move on. If your big idea isn't in the first paragraph, move it there. If you can't find it, rewrite. Simplicity doesn't mean simplicity of thought. Start by asking yourself what you want the person to do as a result of this writing. Just asking yourself that question can make your communication much clearer.

Use plain English, and be specific. Instead of mentioning "the current situation," explain exactly what it is, whether it's low company morale, or an SEC investigation.

Curb your enthusiasm. Avoid overusing exclamation points, regardless of how energized or friendly you might feel. Choose professional sign-offs like "Best" and "Regards" over the too-cute "xoxo".

Whenever possible, use active verbs instead of passive verbs. Active verbs help to energize your prose. Instead of writing "The meeting was led by Tom," write "Tom led the meeting." Use a straightforward sentence structure—subject, verb, object—that people can read quickly.

Beware of common grammatical mistakes, like subject-verb agreement.

Exercise

Here are some specific tips for good business writing followed by some examples that are not proper in business writing. Revise those sentences to make them appropriate in business writing.

Tip 1: State what to do, not what to avoid.
Never take more than two days to process an order.

Tip 2: Say what you can do, not what you can't do.
We can't meet now. It has to wait until Monday morning.

Tip 3: Use neutral rather than blaming language.
You misunderstood what I said.

Tip 4: Use words that create a positive feeling.
At this company we don't waste natural resources.

Tip 5: Take every opportunity to communicate positively.
We have received your letter.

Tip 6: Use passive voice to avoid blaming someone.
Andy lost the drawings.

Tip 7: Do more with less.
(*The following paragraph contains 70 words. Rewrite it and cut it down to 35 words or less.*)

This document is for the purpose of giving the reader a detailed explanation of the inventory process. It describes the activities we currently do in the majority of instances on a daily and weekly basis. In order to provide an introduction to the process for employees who work on a temporary basis, we also have prepared an overview, which describes the highlights of the inventory process in just two pages.

Part Three Case Study

Companies Outsource Because That's Where the Sales Are

The political war against "off-shoring"—which is what the critics usually mean when they use the term "outsourcing"—is raging this election year, in part because of Democrats' failed efforts to stimulate the economy. But there is an important reason why many U.S. companies open stores, build factories and hire people overseas: That's where the sales are.

General Electric Chief Executive Jeffery Immelt, a close Obama advisor, told the Wall Street Journal last year that 30 percent of GE's business was overseas in 2000; today it's 46 percent, and the majority of GE's employees are now overseas.

Ditto for Caterpillar, whose overseas workforce grew by 39 percent between 2005 and 2010, compared to a 7.8 percent U.S. increase.

A 2011 report from the U.S. Commerce Department says that about a third of the roughly 31 million U.S. employees of multinational firms work abroad-and growing. That's because with only about 4 percent of the world's population and a burgeoning middle class in several heavily populated developing countries, such as Brazil, Russia, India and China, the fastest growing markets are outside the U.S.

But first, let's clear up some of the confusion surrounding the terms. Outsourcing is when a company contracts with an outside person or company to provide some products or services, such as bookkeeping, payroll processing or janitorial services, or more complicated functions like marketing or IT services. And families do the same thing when they turn to professionals for major plumbing, air conditioner or car repairs.

Economists refer to this process of turning to those who can produce a product or service at a lower marginal cost as "comparative advantage," and it's the key ingredient to an efficient and productive economy.

If a company outsources jobs to another country, that's off-shoring. However, companies can also build stores or factories in foreign countries and hire the people who work there. That's also off-shoring, but it isn't necessary outsourcing. Those are company employees, both American and foreign.

From an economic standpoint, it makes no difference whether or not that outsourcing is with a person or firm in the same town, state or country. Economics is unconcerned with national borders; politics, on the other hand, is very concerned, and especially in this economic climate.

Frankly, it isn't entirely clear what the critics of outsourcing, or off-shoring, want to stop. An Obama ad says Mitt Romney "supports tax breaks for companies that ship jobs overseas," and accuses Romney of supporting outsourcing while Obama believes in "insourcing".

But Wal-Mart is opening stores all over the world and hiring people to man them. The Wall Street Journal reports the company added 100 000 employees outside of the U.S. last year. How is the company supposed to staff its stores unless it hires nationals who live there and speak the language? Should Wal-Mart be forced to pay higher taxes, which is what the president wants, for growing and competing overseas?

We used to praise that type of competitive spirit and success—*used to.*

Or take International Paper. The Journal reports that the 114-year-old company is also growing much faster outside the U.S. than at home. Between 2008 and 2011, sales in the U.S. and Europe remained about the same, while sales in Asia more than doubled, to $1.8 billion.

To add insult to injury in Obama's view, International Paper is cutting U.S. jobs and closing factories while expanding overseas. But is that because the company is engaged in some type of corporate tax dodge, as Obama likes to pretend? Uh, no, it seems that Americans are using less paper as their transition to a digital economy, while there is a growing demand for paper in developing countries.

Should International Paper stay land-locked-or insourced, to use the president's term—to avoid the extra taxes and accusations of being unpatriotic?

Yes, some U.S. companies produce their products overseas in order to take advantage of lower labor costs—i.e., comparative advantage. But that means U.S. consumers get cheaper prices. You'll notice no one complained when gasoline prices recently fell, even though much of that oil is produced overseas. The public was elated because lower gas prices means more money left over to spend on other wants and needs. Well, the exact same reasoning applies to manufactured goods, raw materials and other products and services that U.S. consumers buy for less because of lower foreign costs.

Of course, some off-shoring efforts have not worked as well as others. U.S. customers often get frustrated when they are connected to a call-center person whose English is barely understandable. And that negative customer experience has forced some companies to reevaluate their off-shoring strategy.

In addition, Washington needs to understand that some off-shoring is a justifiable response to the quickly escalating number of government regulations, especially under the Obama administration, and the highest corporate tax rate in the developed world.

But instead of reducing regulations and creating a tax structure that rewards U.S. companies' efforts to grow and enter new markets, most Democrats' anti-outsourcing demagoguery only demonizes and punishes them.

It's almost as if these off-shoring critics have spent their whole lives as community organizers rather than business owners. Had they run a business they might have a better idea how to run a country?

A. *Answer the following questions:*
1) Why do companies outsource?
2) Why is outsourcing increasing?
3) In what way do government regulations influence the development of outsourcing industry?

B. *Role play the situation based on the description below.*

> As the members of the management of your company, you are holding a meeting discussing "What are the key areas of my business that I should think about outsourcing to save money without causing any issues in customer service?"

Unit Two

Managing Culture in Outsourcing

Note on the topic

软件外包已经成为中国软件产业发展的一个重要方向。承接国际软件外包业务有利于提高中国软件企业的成熟度和国际化水平。跨文化沟通,合作方的能力,合作方的信誉,外包合同规范性,双方交往经验,对合作方人员的信任等因素影响着软件外包的成功与否。在软件外包领域,发包方和承包方在进行任何跨文化和跨地区协作时,都必须首先考虑地域和文化差异。除此之外,企业之间也存在文化差异。

跨文化沟通在外包行业有怎样的重要性?企业之间存在怎样的文化差异?这些就是本章将要讨论的问题。

Part One Reading

I. Before you read

A. Discuss the following questions in a group.

1) What is coding?
2) Is there any difference between coding and programming?

B. Skim the text and answer the following questions:

1) What is culture?
2) What is corporate culture?
3) Why cross culture communication is important in outsourcing services?

II. Text Reading

Avoiding Culture Clash in Outsourced Services

Two facility executives meet at a conference on facility management best practices. When they strike up a conversation, they find they both have outsourced a major facilities function within the past year. As they compare notes on their experiences, one executive **touts** his roaring success with the new outsourcing partnership, while the other laments a situation **fraught** with service and personnel problems.

The experiences of outsourcing efforts are as varied as the **vendors** providing the services, and no single factor accounts for the **discrepancies** in outsourcing relationships. But one ingredient that often is overlooked in finding the right outsourcing mix is corporate culture. Understanding the tremendous impact corporate culture has on the success or failure of outsourcing can help facility executives avoid the **pitfalls** associated with a bad arrangement.

To find a good fit between an outsource firm and an organization, it is essential to understand what corporate culture means. There are many definitions for the term—from the formal one in the dictionary to the most informal ones voiced during focus group sessions with facility executives. Here are three **apt** descriptions:

- Culture is the sum total of ways of living built up by a group of human beings and transmitted from one generation to another;
- Culture is the values shared by the people in a group that tend to persist over time even when group membership changes, and the behavior patterns or style of an organization that new employees are automatically encouraged to follow by their fellow employees; and
- Culture is the way things get done around this place.

Culture is the very **essence** of a company's DNA. It can be considered the company's **genes**, personality, norms and values that often aren't captured formally in documents or processes. Yet culture is the cement that holds a company together. The larger and more established the institution, the more **entrenched** and inflexible the culture tends to be.

Contrast that sort of corporate culture with the culture of an outsourcing firm, which, by the very nature of its business, has to be the **antithesis** of an older, more established corporate culture. To compete successfully in the marketplace, companies in the outsourcing business have to be fast-moving, **dynamic** and **fluid**, and have highly adaptable structures designed to change rapidly as new customer demands arise. Unless an outsource firm has a history and previous existence before it became a service provider, its culture is by design less well-defined and embedded within the organization.

The potential for a clash of these two cultures is clear. If an outsource firm and a prospective client company do not walk and talk the same cultural language from the beginning of the relationship, the two organizations end up working at cross purposes. The outsource firm doesn't fit into the corporate environment and the corporate environment can't work with the culture the outsource firm brings to the client.

For facility executives to secure the proper fit between cultures when they are searching for a service provider, they should do extensive homework at the front end of the **solicitation** and selection process while preparing their internal customer population for the change that is about to occur. In other words, striking a match between an external service provider, and the corporate constituents is all about relationship building and changing management. What follows are guidelines to help determine whether an external service provider will be a good fit for the organization.

From the moment an organization determines a service or function is going to be outsourced, facility executives should involve customer groups and senior management in the outsourcing process. It's important to have an outsourcing **steering** committee comprised of key customers and critical management organization representatives. The role of the steering committee is twofold: to help determine what attributes an outsource firm needs to possess to be successful within the company; and to **syndicate** the risk for the facility management organization in selecting a firm to be the service provider. Throughout the process, steering committee representatives serve as advisers to the facilities staff on everything, from establishing the components of the **RFP** to develop the evaluation and selection criteria.

Once prospective **bidders** submit their proposals, the steering committee also participates in evaluating and selecting a vendor. Having customers involved in the outsourcing process from the day one creates a stake for them in the outcome. At the same time, steering committee members help to sell the service provider concept to their respective organizations and pave the way for the transition in service delivery.

Before the RFP is actually written, facility executives should talk with colleagues that have good working relationships with their providers. Talking with colleagues in the same industry as well as those in unrelated industries is important. The essence of what is being explored is the relationship with the provider, not the industry they serve. Communicating with others allows facility executives to explore and pre-qualify potential outsource firms based on the experience of others. Through this research, facility executives can eliminate some firms from consideration and identify those they want to invite to participate in the competitive process.

(849 words)

Ⅲ. Words to Note

tout	vt.	兜售;招徕
fraught	adj.	充满的,满载的
vendor	n.	供应商
discrepancy	n.	矛盾;不符合(之处)
pitfall	n.	陷阱;圈套;诱惑
apt	adj.	恰当的,适当的
essence	n.	本质,实质;精华
gene	n.	<生>基因;遗传因子
entrenched	adj.	根深蒂固的,牢固的,固守的

续表

antithesis	n.	对立；对立面；对照；对偶
dynamic	adj.	动态的,不断变化的,充满变数的
fluid	adj.	易变的,不固定的
solicitation	n.	诱惑；游说
steering	n.	指导
syndicate	v.	把(新闻或电视节目)同时出售给多家媒体(供其发表或播放)
bidder	n.	出价者,投标人
RFP	abbr.	(request for proposal)招标书

Ⅳ. Part of Reading Section

Read the text and answer the following questions.

1) What are the cultural differences between outsourcing companies and those with long established corporate culture?

2) Why is it important to involve customer groups and senior management in the outsourcing process?

3) What are the functions of the steering committee?

4) What will happen when an outsource firm and a prospective client company are culturally unfit?

5) How important it is to build relationship with providers?

Ⅴ. Vocabulary Building

A. *Match the words with their definitions.*

1.	fluid	a.	used to describe a process that constantly changes and progresses
2.	vendor	b.	the act of enticing a person to do something wrong
3.	essence	c.	unstable and is likely to change often
4.	dynamic	d.	firmly established, so that it would be difficult to change it
5.	solicitation	e.	basic and most important characteristic which gives something its individual identity
6.	entrenched	f.	be filled with
7.	pitfall	g.	a person who owns and sells things
8.	fraught with	h.	an unforeseen or unexpected or surprising difficulty

B. Complete sentence with the words given.

| essence | fluid | fraught with | pitfall |
| entrenched | solicitation | dynamic | vendor |

1) When a body is immersed in a _____, it apparently loses weight.

2) We must try to get to the _____ of things.

3) Sexism is deeply _____ in our society.

4) If any information contained in this email involves any securities or financial products, it shall not be construed as an offer, _____ or sale thereof, nor shall it guarantee any earnings.

5) He knew I was energetic and _____ and would get things done.

6) Export promotion is _____ danger.

7) NSN isn't the only major _____ benefiting from the growing trend for carrier outsourcing.

8) Another _____ for real-estate investors: not accounting for unexpected expenses.

C. Which of the following words can be used to describe a company's character? Write them in the box below.

aggressive	conservative	curious	critical	energetic
friendly	articulate	enthusiastic	easygoing	tolerant
isolated	aggressive	lively	outgoing	honest
innovative	logical	ambitious	sensitive	sarcastic
open	optimistic	pessimistic	rude	shy
warm	rebellious	straightforward	independent	confident
cynical	intelligent	gentle	sympathetic	logical
mature	tough-minded	talkative	outspoken	big-headed

D. Translate the following paragraph into Chinese.

Culture is the very essence of a company's DNA. It can be considered the company's genes, personality, norms and values that often aren't captured formally in documents or processes. Yet culture is the cement that holds a company together. The larger and more established the institution, the more entrenched and inflexible the culture tends to be.

VI. Further Reading

Managing Culture When Outsourcing

India is one of the most popular countries to which to outsource—so much that it has been described as the "back office of the world". Here, the English language is spoken widely and the hierarchical culture lends itself to employees following instructions and call scripts very well. However, there are many differences between Western and Asian cultures that can present problems if not managed proactively.

Communication is one of the main problems. Although both Western and Asian teams, for example, can speak fluent English, the use of language can be so different that miscommunication can result. A Swiss manager recently visited a call centre in India and was surprised at the number of staff in the building. He asked if he could take a photograph. His Indian counterpart said: "It is too crowded now." This was his way of saying "no". Western managers need to learn to read between the lines of the subtle and indirect use of language in Asian cultures.

The word "yes" can also be misunderstood. If you ask an Indian employee "can you complete this report by tomorrow?" they will usually say "yes". However, in reality, "yes" can mean "I hear you" or "maybe".

Cultural attitudes towards "time" also need addressing. Time is viewed in a different way and is not always a priority in Asian cultures, for example, where building good relationships is generally more important. It is for this reason, many non-Western cultures may not prioritize time, so keeping a customer "on-hold" for ten minutes will be seen as normal and not be perceived as an issue at all. Unless being trained appropriately and sufficiently, staff may continue to believe "it just doesn't matter". Strict guidelines and enforcement may also be necessary to adhere to western style fixed deadlines.

In addition, non-Western societies place importance on hierarchy, which means an employee would not want to lose face in front of his or her boss and so may appear to agree to complete a task such as to finish a report. When it is not completed, the Western manager understandably feels frustrated. But what might be the view of the employee?

In fact, the employee will feel frustrated and unsupported as they were not asked additional questions, such as: Do you have the resources to prepare the report by tomorrow? Do you have the report template? Do you have the licensed software to run the report? The level of micro-management may need to be much higher to ensure successful delivery of any task. One way to achieve this is to learn how a manager representative of a given culture would work with his or her staff.

(443 words)

A. Give brief answers to the following questions:

1) What are the aspects of cultural difference between India and the west mentioned in the

text?

2) What problems are resulted from miscommunications?

3) Do you think Chinese culture is similar to Indian culture? If so, in what way are they in common?

B. *Group work*: ***What suggestions you would like to Chinese outsourcing companies based on the text you have read? Discuss in a group and list your points below.***

_____
_____
_____
_____
_____
_____

Cultural Notes

Every workplace has a culture, and no two are ever alike. A company's culture often reflects the operating tastes, preferences, and style of the company's chief executive. He or she ultimately sets the tone and shapes the work environment. Quite simply, the corporate culture is the operating work environment that is set and shaped by the executive:

- The way people dress.
- The way people act (both on and off the job).
- The way people present themselves.
- The way people conduct their work.
- The way supervisors are encouraged to manage departments.
- The way customers are treated and served.
- The way workers interact with supervisors.
- The way workers interact with each other.
- The way people interact across departments.
- The way people interact with the public.
- The way business is conducted and done.

Individually and collectively, these factors will likely determine if a company is right for you, or if you are right for the company.

As you'll no doubt discover, corporate cultures evolve over time, and workplace environments often change, sometimes significantly, whenever a new executive takes the helm. During such times, everyone, from top executives on down, must adapt and adjust to new ways of doing business. How well you're able to adapt to the changes in the work environment will also affect your overall happiness and success at the company.

Part Two Writing

Writing skills: Process of Business Writing

I. Plan

Planning is a series of strategies designed to find and formulate information in writing. It helps you uncover, explore and evaluate a topic. It helps you locate and produce information in writing.

1) Choose your channels.

How important is the message?
How much feedback is required?
How fast is feedback needed?
Is a permanent record necessary?
How much can be spent?
How formal and confidential is the message?

2) Writer's purpose: why are you writing?

To inquire	To invite
To request	To follow up
To acknowledge	To apply for a job
To remind	To resign

3) Reader's response: What do you want the readers to do?

Different writing situations and assignments require different voices.

Readers tend to be most comfortable with an even tone of voice, a style that values the middle and avoids the extremes of the impersonal or the intimate, the long-winded or the curt, and the stuffy or the casual.

4) Reader's information: What do you want your readers to know?

Developing Readers' Benefits and "You" View

"I" and "We" View	"You" View
We take pleasure in announcing an agreement we made with HP to allow us to offer discounted printers in the student store	An agreement with HP allows you and other students to buy discounted printers at your convenient student store
We are issuing a refund	You will receive a refund
We need your account number before we can do anything	Would you mind giving me your account number so that I can find your records and help you solve this problem
I have a few questions on which I would like feedback	Your feedback is important. Please answer a few questions

II. Exercise

Please identify WHY, WHAT and WHAT in the following email.

Subject: Sales Skills Training Information

Dear Sir/Madam:

I am the training manager for Real People. We specialize in finding Temporary employees for companies.

We are interested in learning more about your sales skills training program and would like to know the following by Friday. We plan on choosing a Training company next week.

1. Training programs
2. Pricing for long term training and a two-day workshop
3. Number of people allowed in the training course

Thank you, and let me know if you need any additional information.

Regards,
Albert Wang

Your Answer:

Why is Albert writing?

_____

What does he want the readers to do?

_____

What does he want the readers to know?

_____

III. Organize

1) Types of correspondence:

Internal correspondence — the message you write to colleague: email, fax and memo.

External correspondence — the message you write to customers: email, fax, and letter.

2) Organizing: SOFAR Strategy.

Salutation	Dear Mr/Mrs/Ms/Miss...
Opening	Background + Purpose
Facts	Reader's Information
Action	Reader's Response
Remarks	Polite Closing

Identify SOFAR in the following email.

Dear Mr Lin,

Thank you for your email of 9 March. In the email, you mentioned that you had sent a cheque to settle your VISA Card Annual Fee.

I would like to explain the situation.

We have checked our records carefully. Unfortunately, we have not yet received the cheque, although we are normally very efficient when dealing with incoming remittances.

Therefore, to help us prepare your new VISA Card, we would be grateful if you could settle the payment immediately.

We look forward to hearing from you soon.

Yours sincerely,
Kevin Chen
Customer Service Manager

IV. Revise

Revising is a series of strategies designed to reexamine and reevaluate the choices that have created a piece of writing.

- Use simple language.

Use	Do not use
please	will you be good enough to
prefer	express a preference for
because	for the reason that
ask	request
buy	purchase
need	request
do	accomplish

- Formal & informal language.

Formal	Informal
approximately	about
inquire	ask
ascertain	find out
obtain	receive
assist	help
participate	share
construct	build
purchase	buy
contribute	give
sufficient	enough
difficult	hard
utilize	use

- Avoid Wordy Expressions and Unnecessary Repetition.

Wordy	Concise
We would like to	Please
A long period of time	A long time
I expect it to be	Expected
During the year of 2008	During 2008
For the development of	For developing
Squaring shape	Square
During the time that	While

V. Exercise

Rearrange the paragraphs and lay the letter out correctly. Print a draft, proof read, make any final corrections and print a final copy.

	I look forward to hearing from you in the near future
	Yours faithfully
	I purchased a whizzy wonder mobile phone from you in November of last year at a cost of £ 150

	The phone has never worked properly and I have taken it back to Dixet many times for repair
	The Manager, Dixet Electricals, East Road, Sudnorth, Suffolk IP54 6ED
	Smith Phone number 01787 546987
	I am writing to complain about my mobile phone
	Dear Sir
	I would like to receive a full refund of the cost of this phone or a new replacement. I do not want a further repair
	John A. Smith
	Each time the phone has been brought back to you it has been impossible to trace the fault
	although your staff agree that it does not work properly

Part Three Case Study

ROBERT GIBSON demonstrates how a German-Chinese team can face intercultural problems—and explains how to deal with them, and how to avoid them.

On the surface, this highly successful joint venture in the electronic industries is going well. Research and Development (R&D) is based in Germany, and production is based in China. The business is starting to be profitable. But tensions develop in the team, and an external consultant is brought in to analyze the situation. This is what she reports after interviewing representatives from both sides. Think about what advice you would give to each team and then compare your comments.

The German manager's view of the Chinese

"We are impressed by our ambitious Chinese colleagues and their speedy reactions. They seem keen to learn and are very open-minded. What is not so good is that they aren't prepared to take responsibility or follow agreed procedures. They think in a hierarchical way and there is very little horizontal communication. They seem reluctant to take the initiative or make independent decisions. Recently, they have started to turn up late to meetings or not come at all. When we ask them about a problem, they often beat about the bush, and it is very difficult to know what they are really thinking. They smile politely and say yes, but don't do anything. I wish they'd put their cards on the table and tell us directly if they have a problem with something. We've hired quite a few new Chinese colleagues but, although they have excellent qualifications on paper, we've been disappointed with their performance. The other issue is loyalty. We hire them, train them and then they leave and join one of our competitors."

The Chinese manager's view of the Germans

"The Germans are excellent planners, and they think very logically. We like their focus on quality and their disciplined, straightforward approach. They like China and clearly enjoy themselves when they come to see us in Shanghai. On the other hand, they don't seem to trust us. They don't give us any real responsibility. Instead, they set up complicated processes that just slow everything down and stop us from reaching our targets. They waste time with too many meetings. They are never available when we need them—you can rarely get them at the weekend and they often seem to be away on holiday. If we can't get an answer to our questions quickly, we have a problem with the deadlines that they have set for us and keep insisting on. Also, some of the teams have been shocked by the way the Germans behave in their free time in China. Maybe there are too many temptations in Shanghai. They complain about the Chinese stealing Western know-how but, at the same time, if they have a few hours free before their flight to Germany, they go to the fake market and buy watches and clothing for their family and friends."

I. Team activity

You work for a consulting company. A foreign firm is seeking a business partner in China to outsource their products. You need to introduce a Chinese company in the outsourcing industry. What do you need to know about the corporate culture? What do they need to know about Chinese culture? How can they get well along with Chinese employees?

A. *Introduction to the company in China.*
- What is the average cost of the company's product or service?
- How many people currently work for the company?
- What are the company's annual profits?
- How competitive the company is in the outsourcing industry in China?

B. *Introduction to the Chinese Culture.*
- What is the physical environment like?
- What kinds of religious traditions do the people follow?
- What cultural rituals do they engage in?
- What kinds of foods do the people eat?
- What do people do for entertainment?
- How do people get their news? Are there restrictions on the kind of information or news they are allowed to receive?
- What is the average income for local workers?
- Are there any cultural taboos in the Chinese culture?

II. Assignment

Reflecting on what you learned from the group work, in groups, you will draft and present in class your report which contains the following information:

- Overview of the company.
- Statement of purpose.
- Statement about how the foreign company would benefit from doing business with the Chinese company.
- Statement of opportunities and challenges.
- Cultural considerations the company has addressed.

Unit Three

Handling Clients

Note on the topic

你们都遇到过这样的问题：那就是让你如同生活在地狱里的客户们！他们总是心急火燎地让你交作品，怀疑你的一切合理化建议。他们一来电话，一进你的办公室，一给你发邮件，你就感觉头痛，因为你知道麻烦又来了！这一章里就让我们一起来探讨一下如何跟客户保持良好的合作关系，如何正确对待和处理客户麻烦的要求，如何让外包双方都能愉快地完成各自的工作！

Part One   Reading

I. Before you read

A. *Class Activity*: "*Let me tell you what I can do！*"

- Purpose: To illustrate the importance of telling people what you can do but not what you can't.
- Goal: To help participants think creatively about how they can avoid saying no.
- Direction: The whole class could be divided into group of 6. Each group please makes the members stand in a circle. Tell each of them that they will ask another member of the class for something that he or she cannot say yes to. That person must then come up with an appropriate response. When that round is complete, the responder then makes a request of someone else.

For example:

Member 1 to member 2: "I want rolled Sushi（寿司）for lunch."

Member 2 to member 1: "The cafeteria has a variety of options. But I've never found Sushi on the menu. They do have wonderful fried rice with seafood. How about that?"

Member 1: "Okay, that sounds nice！"

Member 2 to member 3: "..."

- Remember: Try to make your request wired and funny. When you respond to a request, try to be creative and have fun!

B. Discuss within small groups about The Important Factors that will make a good relationship between the outsourcer and the contractor. Make a list of your points.

e. g. be professional, good communication...

C. Skim the text and answer or discuss the following questions:

1) How many suggestions are provided by the writer in order to make clients happy? What are they?

_____

2) Without looking at the detailed explanation of each suggestion, please briefly state your understanding of each suggestion.

_____

II. Text Reading

Keys To Successful Outsourcing: How To Make Your Clients Happy

Ever feel like your outsourcing partner just doesn't "get" you, your product or your business? Having worked with many different outsourcers across a few different industries, I have developed a good sense of what makes a good partner. Here are a few things I wish all outsourcers understood about how to make clients happy.

1. Do Your Homework

While your client wants you to respond quickly, nothing is more frustrating than receiving work that wasn't wanted in the first place. Take some time to understand the product and the services your client wants from you. Investing a day up front will save days of grief later. Go through the package of work and ask good questions, especially if there is anything that wasn't expected. Hold a kick-off meeting with your client. Find out what is important to your client and the product. Ask for and analyze previous examples and share what you learned, just to make sure you are on the same page. If there are no previous examples, create one from the work you have been asked to do and establish that as the benchmark.

2. Check Your Assumptions

This is particularly important during contract negotiation because no one likes hearing "it's not in the contract" after it has been signed. Even throughout the project, communicate often and check your assumptions as you go. It's better to spend a few minutes checking in than having to redo a bunch of work because the assumption was wrong. Work with your client to set up a schedule for regular communications to make sure you talk more than just when "things come up".

3. Help Us Help You

Good customer service practices tell you to adapt to whatever your customer wants. While it is important to be flexible and adapt, there naturally has to be a limit to still be able to work effectively. As an outsourcing partner, you have the benefit of working with many different clients and learning what works or doesn't work for your team. Understand what are your best practices and don't be afraid to suggest them to your clients. As long as you use templates and practices as a starting point, rather than a required form of bureaucracy, there is a good chance we may appreciate the suggestion. If you need anything from your client to work better, ask for it. Do not assume that we know what you need.

4. Be Transparent And Ask For The Same

While you never want your clients to know about all your dirty laundry, you are kidding yourself if you think that your client can't see when something is wrong. We can tell if you are balancing multiple projects, having problems with the work or experiencing staffing problems. May as well be professional, let your client know about your challenges, what you are doing about it and if there is anything you need from your client to help you succeed. On the same token, you also know when your client is stressed, unhappy or less responsive than usual. Ask if they can share what is going on and find out if there is anything you can do to help. Knowing what is happening on your client's side will also help you adapt your services to their needs.

5. Learn The Language

Every company, every industry uses particular words, acronyms and phrases. Sometimes one word or phrase means different things to different people. Learn your client's lingo and be sure to explain any particular words or phrases you use. If you are working with clients in other countries, it is best to use plain, simple English (or your common working language). Avoid slang and colloquialisms. Otherwise you will spend all your time, just trying to figure out what everyone is talking about.

(638 Words)

Ⅲ. Words to Note

invest	v.	投资,花费
kick-off	n.	开始,启动
analyze	v.	分析
previous	a.	之前的
benchmark	n.	基准点
negotiation	n.	协商
assumption	n.	假设,设想
flexible	a.	灵活的,可协调的

Unit Three　Handling Clients

续表

template	n.	模式,模版
bureaucracy	n.	官僚机构
acronym	n.	首字母缩略词
lingo	n.	术语
plain	a.	清晰的,明白的
slang	n.	俚语
colloquialism	n.	俗语,口语

Ⅳ. Text Understanding

Read the text and answer the following questions.

1) How to "do your homework" before starting the project?
_____

2) Is it necessary to adapt to whatever your client wants? Why or why not?
_____

3) What does "be transparent" mean?
_____

4) What shall we pay special attention to when communicating with clients from another country?
_____

5) Which of the suggestions do you think is the most important one? Why?
_____

Ⅴ. Vocabulary Building

A. *Choose an appropriate word in the box to complete the sentences below. Change the form when necessary.*

negotiation	assumption	lingo	previous
invest	analyze	flexible	template

1) Most companies offer _____ working so that employees can choose from a variety of methods that fit them best.

2) Economics is easy after you learn the _____.

3) Do you have any _____ experience of this type of work?

4) The _____ with the company had reached a crucial stage.

5) Her childhood became a _____ for how she brought up her own children.

6) Oliver made a fortune by _____ in antique furniture.

7) My calculations were based on the _____ that house prices would remain steady.

8) You need to sit down and _____ why you feel so upset.

B. *Understand the idioms—Please write down your explanations of the following idiomatic expressions in the text.*

1) Kick-off meeting: _____

2) on the same page: _____

3) dirty laundry: _____

4) on the same token: _____

C. *Learn more idioms—Try this fun quiz to check your understanding of English idioms.*

1) A jack of all trades.

For which job would a jack of all trades be best suited?

a) A dealer in a casino.

b) A caretaker in a school.

c) A teller in a bank.

2) Back to the drawing board.

We started an online business, but after a while it was back to the drawing board because

a) we couldn't make a profit.

b) we made a lot of money.

c) we wanted to improve our drawing.

3) Dig up dirt.

A journalist is digging up dirt on a politician in order to

a) help the politician's campaign.

b) damage the politician's image.

c) increase the politician's popularity.

4) Fly off the handle.

We were having dinner in a restaurant last night when this guy at the next table flew off the handle because

a) the food was so delicious.

b) the waiter was so handsome.

c) the waiter brought the wrong thing.

5) Have a soft spot for.

You can see that Mike's got a soft spot for dogs. Whenever he sees one, he

a) kicks it.

b) pats it on the head.

c) keeps away from it.

6) Leave no stone unturned.

Henry said he'd leave no stone unturned in his search for a woman to marry. He will

a) look for women under stones.

b) try everything to find a wife.

c) marry any woman who accepts him.

7) Ring a bell.

When I heard the poem, some of the lines rang a bell and

a) some of them beat a drum.

b) sounded very beautiful.

c) I thought I'd heard it somewhere before.

8) Take the plunge.

Monique has decided to take the plunge and

a) keep her job for a while.

b) start up her own business.

c) put all her money in the bank.

9) Up in the air.

We'll have to leave the list of guests we're inviting to our wedding up in the air until we know

a) how many we can invite.

b) what the weather will be like.

c) if any are of them are afraid of heights.

10) You could have knocked me over with a feather.

You could have knocked me over with a feather when I heard that

a) we were having sandwiches for lunch.

b) the electricity bill had arrived.

c) I had won a million dollars in the lottery.

D. *Please translate the following paragraph into Chinese.*

Good customer service practices tell you to adapt to whatever your customer wants. While it is important to be flexible and adapt, there naturally has to be a limit to still be able to work effectively. As an outsourcing partner, you have the benefit of working with many different clients and learning what works or doesn't work for your team. Understand what are your best practices and don't be afraid to suggest them to your clients. As long as you use templates and practices as a starting point, rather than a required form of bureaucracy, there is a good chance we may appreciate the suggestion. If you need anything from your client to work better, ask for it. Do not assume that we know what you need.

Ⅵ. Further Reading

Four Brilliant Ways to Handle Client Changes You Don't Want to Make

Let's say you've spent hours on designing a website mockup for a new client, only to have a huge list of changes sent back that will for sure ruin your work. Have you ever dealt with a client situation like this? It could be a simple color change that doesn't go well together, or they may want to have you add an audio clip that automatically plays over their website. I've dealt with some situations like that... it was not fun!

Here's a specific situation I remember having with a past client:

"Can you move the website's navigation from the top and put it vertically on the right side? I spent a great deal of time investigating website design and did an informal presentation of this. Everyone liked the buttons on the right."

They spent a great deal of time *investigating* website design?!

This was a real "client from hell" situation where every email from them made me cringe. They had no real training in graphic design, and I'm guessing they "investigated" in all the wrong places due to the revisions they would ask for. Unfortunately you might find yourself in one of these sticky client situations, and you'll need to know how to handle it. The solutions below can give you an idea of how to handle a situation like this, but may be easier read than done—seeing that every situation is unique.

1. Explain your solution and educate the client

Stay calm, stay positive and don't take their feedback personally. Use this as a chance to educate the client. Explain to the client why their changes might not be best, and what your solution (as the professional) is for the situation. Always try to respond with confidence and show them that you're reliable.

If there's a problem that arises, be sure that your response is always solution-oriented (and not defensive). You don't want to complicate the situation and client relationship. It's more than likely that the client will understand, value your professional input and go with what you think is best. BUT what happens when you're dealing with a stubborn client? In this case, you'll need to take your input a bit further...

2. Give factual data that proves your solution is best

If your client is a hardheaded person then it might be best to backup your input with some proof that shows your solution is best. The easiest way to do this would be to mock it up. Actually show the client why your solution is best.

Another way to sway their thoughts would be to provide reputable sources, i.e. other websites with a usable layout, a print design with proper white space, etc. Tell them to spend a few minutes using/reading those sources. This might help educate them in your solution.

Again, whatever you do, try not to argue or respond defensively if the client still stands by their decision. Remember that it's ultimately their project, and you want them to be happy with the final result.

3. Do your best to work with the changes

Not every project you take on will be portfolio worthy (it's the honest truth), and sometimes you just have to work with the client's ideas to please them. If they're happy—you're happy.

Due to the client's stubbornness, if the final result is completely horrifying, you might want to do a couple of things:

As with every client project, keep a copy of all dialog exchanged between you and them. This way, if the client gets any complaints about how terrible their website's usability is or how hard it is to read their copy, you have something to use as a backstop.

The second thing that you might want to do is pull your name or brand from the project (like a website footer). If you don't enjoy the project, then you can choose not to take credit for it.

Again, I can't stress how important it is that you keep your communication with the client professional. You don't want to burn any bridges, even if you don't plan on working with them in the future.

4. Let go or pass on the project

This solution is a bit drastic, but if you are completely against the client's changes, then you have every right to back out.

Be completely honest when discussing this with the client. Whether you don't believe in the work they're having you produce or if you can't seem to be apart of a project that goes against everything, you're trying to make better in your field of work.

Again, try to respond in a solution-oriented manner. Give them your best input and they can move forward with their project taking your advice or not.

Or...

Recommend the project to someone else willing to take it on. (It might be smart to give that person a heads up before they waste any time as you might have.)

(836 Words)

A. *Please fill in the blanks with an appropriate word or expression from the text.*

Sometimes, when the client wants to change the colors that don't _____ _____ together or add an _____ _____ plays over the website, you might feel that your design has been _____. Whenever you find yourself in a _____ client situation, you need to _____ it. First, you need to stay _____ and always try to respond with _____. Try to explain to your client that your solution is more _____ with a _____ attitude but not defensive. If the client is too _____, keep a copy of _____ between you, pull your name or _____ from the project, and keep _____ professionally. If you are completely against the changes, be _____ with your client or you could recommend the project to someone else who wants to _____ _____ the job.

B. *Match the following English expressions with the Chinese Explanations.*

Column A	Column B
1. Website mockup	a. 平面设计
2. Audio clip	b. 提醒
3. Graphic design	c. 音频
4. Solution-oriented	d. 反对
5. Hardheaded	e. 邀功
6. Backstop	f. 网站模型
7. Take credit	g. 推出
8. Back out	h. 为了解决问题的
9. Go against	i. 支撑
10. Heads up	j. 顽固的

Cultural Notes

WHAT ARE EFFECTIVE COMMUNICATIONS FOR RESOLVING COMPLAINTS?

There are definitely effective and ineffective communication methods for dealing with complaints. A base level rule is that "personal is better". If it is at all possible, you are better to resolve a complaint by talking to the person face to face. The worst complaint resolution processes are the dehumanising, take a number, "we will get to you when we have time" approach.

It should be clear that workers must be able to demonstrate some essential skills before being given any role in a complaint resolution process.

Those essential skills should include the ability to:
- let the customer know they have your full attention.
- listen and develop a clear understanding of what the complaint is about.
- acknowledge the problem and be empathetic and calm to help alleviate the customer's stress.
- take notes without filtering or interpreting the information.
- ask questions to clarify or expand knowledge of the complaint.

- give the customer opportunities to ask questions. Tell the customer you want to help improve the situation. Ask how they would like to proceed.
- explain how the complaint procedure works.
- ensure the customer is comfortable with the process. Decide what can be done to fix the problem and tell them.
- contact the customer within an agreed time-frame to ensure the problem was resolved.
- maintain a courteous and professional approach.

Part Two Writing

Writing Skills: How to write a complaint letter?

Writing a letter of complaint is something most people have to do at some point in their lives. Whether you're dissatisfied with a company's product or service, it is usually possible to resolve the issue in a mutually beneficial way through a firm but polite letter of complaint. Writing a complaint letter should not be complicated or scary—all you need to do is clearly state the facts and politely request a resolution.

How to Write a Complaint Letter?

- Include your name, address, and home and work phone numbers.
- Type your letter if possible. If it is handwritten, make sure it is neat and easy to read.
- Make your letter brief and to the point. Include all important facts about your purchase, including the date and place where you made the purchase and any information you can give about the product or service such as serial or model numbers or specific type of service.
- State exactly what you want done about the problem and how long you are willing to wait to get it resolved. Be reasonable.
- Include all documents regarding your problem. Be sure to send COPIES, not originals.
- Avoid writing an angry, sarcastic, or threatening letter. The person reading your letter probably was not responsible for your problem but may be very helpful in resolving it.
- Keep a copy of the letter for your records.

I. Template of Complaint Letter

_____ Name of Contact Person (if available)
_____ Title (if available)
_____ Company Name
Consumer Complaint Division (if you have no contact person)
_____ Street Address, City, State, Zip Code

Dear _____ (Contact Person):

Re: _____ (account number, if applicable)

On _____ (date), I _____ (bought, leased, rented, or had repaired) a _____ (name of the product, with serial or model number or service performed) at _____ (location and other important details of the transaction).

Unfortunately, your product (or service) has not performed well (or the service was inadequate) because _____ (state the problem). I am disappointed because _____ (explain the problem: for example, the product does not work properly, the service was not performed correctly, I was billed the wrong amount, something was not disclosed clearly or was misrepresented, etc.).

To resolve the problem, I would appreciate it if you could _____ (state the specific action you want—money back, charge card credit, repair, exchange, etc.). Enclosed are copies of my records (include copies of receipts, guarantees, warranties, canceled checks, contracts, model and serial numbers, and any other documents).

I look forward to your reply and a resolution to my problem, and will wait until _____ (set a time limit) before seeking help from a consumer protection agency or the Better Business Bureau. Please contact me at the above address or by phone at _____ (home and/or office numbers with area code).

Sincerely,

_____ Your name ? Enclosure(s)

cc: (reference to whom you are sending a copy of this letter, if anyone)

II. Sample Letter

56 Disgruntled Street
Somewhere Unhappy
1AM MAD

Customer Service Manager
That Awful Company Somewhere Awful UR BAD
June 15, 2008

Dear Sir/Madam,

I am writing today to complain of the poor service I received from your company on June 12, 2008. I was visited by a representative of That Awful Company, Mr. Madman, at my home on that day.

> Mr. Madman was one hour late for his appointment and offered nothing by way of apology when he arrived at noon. Your representative did not remove his muddy shoes upon entering my house, and consequently left a trail of dirt in the hallway. Mr. Madman then proceeded to present a range of products to me that I had specifically told his assistant by telephone I was not interested in. I repeatedly tried to ask your representative about the products that were of interest to me, but he refused to deal with my questions. We ended our meeting after 25 minutes without either of us having accomplished anything.
>
> I am most annoyed that I wasted a morning (and half a day's vacation) waiting for Mr. Madman to show up. My impression of That Awful Company has been tarnished, and I am now concerned about how my existing business is being managed by your firm. Furthermore, Mr. Madman's inability to remove his muddy shoes has meant that I have had to engage the services, and incur the expense, of a professional carpet cleaner.
>
> I trust this is not the way That Awful Company wishes to conduct business with valued customers—I have been with you since the company was founded and have never encountered such treatment before. I would welcome the opportunity to discuss matters further and to learn of how you propose to prevent a similar situation from recurring. I look forward to hearing from you.
>
> Yours faithfully,
> *V. Angry*
> V. Angry

III. Writing Task

You have bought a new mobile phone and in a few days after purchasing it has stopped working. You spoke to the company representative one week ago but the phone has still not been repaired.

Write a letter to the company. In your letter:
- Introduce yourself.
- Explain the situation.
- Say what action you would like to company to take.

Part Three Case Study

Internet Service Provider Issues

When something goes wrong with an Internet service provider, it can be a tricky business to rectify however determined you are, as this case study demonstrates.

1. Setting Up Broadband Internet

The only downside of Sheila's new flat was that there was no broadband internet connection. As a translator working from home, it was imperative that this was installed set up as soon as possible.

She promptly set up a contract with a local internet service provider. After duly filling in the online form, she was requested to send payment details and a signed confirmation by fax. Once this had been received Sheila was told she could expect to receive her internet within five working days. She waited with great anticipation.

However, instead of receiving the equipment to set up the broadband internet, she received an email informing her that a connection was unavailable at her place of residence.

2. No Account To Cancel

Why hadn't she been told this to begin with? Infuriated, not least by the impersonal template email she received after all the time and effort wasted, she wasted no further time in responding to confirm cancellation of the contract.

Once this was confirmed, she could then look for a new provider. However, the response to this was mystifying—she was told she had no account to cancel. Refusing to accept this perplexing response, she phoned up the company only to be met with the same answer—there was no record of her holding an account.

3. Erroneous Payments

It was tempting to accept the scenario that none of this debacle had actually happened but she was unconvinced. Her suspicions were vindicated when checking her bank account a couple of weeks later, she discovered that the internet service provider had taken payment out of her bank for the supposedly non-existent account.

In response, she immediately phoned up the company to demand an explanation. Frustratingly, she was unable to speak to the company representative from the previous call and had to relate the whole situation to a new call centre operator.

The response she was given was that they couldn't do anything without proof of the erroneous account debit. So Sheila sent a fax confirming the transfer, but unfortunately then failed to receive a response in return, and was forced once again to chase up the complaint.

4. Address Error

This time, after relating the case to another new call centre representative, she was told that the transfer was correct because their records showed that not only had the internet equipment been sent out to Sheila several weeks prior, but it had been received and the broadband duly connected up. Incensed, Sheila insisted that she had never received any equipment and was therefore far from connected.

However, when she asked to confirm the address, to her horror, she discovered that it was a completely different location. It would seem the company had got her payment account details confused with a completely different address, the occupants of which would now be receiving broadband internet at her expense.

The hard work in confirming this administrative error was left to Sheila, who was forced to send a further fax detailing how her home address was different to that receiving an internet connection. Her determined efforts finally paid off when the internet company conceded their error and finally confirmed the cancellation of her account, before refunding the money taken from her bank account in error.

Through her persistent efforts, Sheila had solved the problem. But this case highlights how, even if you're as dogged as she was, it can still be very difficult to resolve certain problems. As the company was found to be entirely in the wrong, Sheila had every right to seek compensation for her time, effort and inconvenience, but, exhausted from her battle for resolution, she decided to let the matter rest.

Group Discussion

Read Sheila's case carefully and discuss the following questions with your group members:

1) What is the biggest frustration Sheila's facing in her campaign? Why?

2) If you were Sheila, how would you deal with this problem?

3) If you were the manager of the help center, what would you do to improve the efficiency of handling clients' problems?

4) In Culture Notes part, you've got some skills of processing customer's complains. If you were one of the call centre representatives who received Sheila's call, what actions should you take to practice those skills? Fill in the table below to describe your action for each of the skills:

Skills	Your Actions/Responses
1) Let the customer know they have your full attention.	
2) Listen and develop a clear understanding of what the complaint is about.	
3) Acknowledge the problem and be empathetic and calm to help alleviate the customer's stress.	
4) Take notes without filtering or interpreting the information.	
5) Ask questions to clarify or expand knowledge of the complaint.	
6) Give the customer opportunities to ask questions. Tell the customer you want to help improve the situation.	
7) Ask how they would like to proceed.	
8) Explain how the complaint procedure works.	
9) Ensure the customer is comfortable with the process. Decide what can be done to fix the problem and tell them.	
10) Contact the customer within an agreed time-frame to ensure the problem was resolved.	
11) Maintain a courteous and professional approach.	

Unit Four

Working Together

Note on the topic

  团队合作是指一群有能力、有信念的人在特定的团队中,为了一个共同的目标相互支持合作奋斗的过程。它可以调动团队成员的所有资源和才智,并且会自动地驱除所有不和谐和不公正现象,同时会给予那些诚心、大公无私的奉献者适当的回报。自觉自愿的团队合作会产生一股强大而且持久的力量。

  所谓团队精神,简单来说就是大局意识、协作精神和服务精神的集中体现。团队精神的基础是尊重个人的兴趣和成就。核心是协同合作,最高境界是全体成员的向心力、凝聚力,反映的是个体利益和整体利益的统一,并进而保证组织的高效率运转。团队精神的形成并不要求团队成员牺牲自我,相反,挥洒个性、表现特长保证了成员共同完成任务目标,而明确的协作意愿和协作方式则产生了真正的内心动力。团队精神是组织文化的一部分,良好的管理可以通过合适的组织形态将每个人安排至合适的岗位,充分发挥集体的潜能。如果没有正确的管理文化,没有良好的从业心态和奉献精神,就不会有团队精神。

Part One Reading

Ⅰ. Before you read

A. *Discuss the following questions in a group.*

1) What is the common theme among those pictures?

2) True or false.

  Some people say "If you want go fast, go alone. If you want to go far, go together". Do you agree with the saying? And give your reasons.

B. *Skim the text and answer the following questions*:

1) Why is it hard to find work places exemplifying team work?

2) What are the powerful actions that can make teamwork happen?

3) How can we put team building into every single day?

II. Text Reading

How to Build a Teamwork Culture

Fostering teamwork is creating a work culture that values **collaboration.** In a teamwork environment, people understand and believe that thinking, planning, decisions and actions are better when done cooperatively. People recognize, and even assimilate, the belief that "none of us is as good as all of us."

It's hard to find work places that **exemplify** teamwork. In America, our institutions such as schools, our family structures, and our pastimes emphasize winning, being the best, and coming out on top. Workers are rarely raised in environments that emphasize true teamwork and collaboration.

Organizations are working on valuing diverse people, ideas, backgrounds, and experiences. We have miles to go before valuing teams and teamwork will be the norm.

You can, however, create a teamwork culture by doing just a few things right. Admittedly, they're hard things, but with commitment and appreciation for the value, you can create an overall sense of teamwork in your organization.

To make teamwork happen, these powerful actions must occur.

Executive leaders communicate the clear expectation that teamwork and collaboration are expected. No one completely owns a work area or process all by himself. People who own work processes and positions are open and receptive to ideas and input from others on the team.

Executives model teamwork in their interaction with each other and the rest of the organization. They maintain teamwork even when things are going wrong and the temptation is to slip back into former team unfriendly behavior.

The organization members talk about and identify the value of a teamwork culture. If values are formally written and shared, teamwork is one of the key five or six.

Teamwork is rewarded and recognized. The lone ranger, even if she is an excellent producer, is valued less than the person who achieves results with others in teamwork. Compensation, bonuses, and rewards depend on collaborative practices as much as individual contribution and achievement.

Important stories and **folklore** that people discuss within the company emphasize teamwork. People who "do well" and are promoted within the company are team players.

The performance management system places emphasis and value on teamwork. Often 360 degree feedback is integrated within the system.

Do you immediately picture your group off at a **resort** playing games or hanging from ropes when you think of team building? Traditionally, many organizations approached team building this way. Then, they wondered why that wonderful sense of teamwork, experienced at the **retreat** or seminar, failed to impact long term beliefs and actions back at work.

I'm not averse to retreats, planning sessions, seminars and team building activities—in fact I lead them—but they have to be part of a larger teamwork effort. You will not build teamwork by "retreating" as a group for a couple of days each year. Think of team building as something you do every single day.

Form teams to solve real work issues and to improve real work processes. Provide training in systematic methods so the team expends its energy on the project, not on figuring out how to work together as a team to approach it.

Hold department meetings to review projects and progress, to obtain broad input, and to coordinate shared work processes. If team members are not getting along, examine the work processes they mutually own. The problem is not usually the personalities of the team members. It's the fact that the team members often haven't agreed on how they will deliver a product or a service or the steps required to get something done.

Build fun and shared occasions into the organization's agenda. Hold pot luck lunches; take the team to a sporting event. Sponsor dinners at a local restaurant. Go hiking or to an **amusement** park. Hold a monthly company meeting. Sponsor sports teams and encourage cheering team fans.

Use ice breakers and teamwork exercises at meetings. I worked with an organization that held a weekly staff meeting. Participants took turns bringing a "fun" ice breaker to the meeting. These activities were limited to ten minutes, but they helped participants laugh together and get to know each other—a small investment in a big time sense of team.

Celebrate team successes publicly. Buy everyone the same t-shirt or hat. Put team member names in a drawing for company **merchandise** and gift certificates. You are limited in teamwork only by your imagination.

Take care of the hard issues above and do the types of teamwork activities listed here. You'll be amazed at the progress you will make in creating a teamwork culture, a culture that enables individuals to contribute more than they ever thought possible—together.

(784 words)

III. Words to Note

foster	v.	培养
collaboration	n.	合作
exemplify	v.	举例说明
folklore	n.	民间传说,民俗
resort	n.	旅游胜地
retreat	n.	休息寓所
amusement	n.	娱乐
merchandise	n.	商品,货物

IV. Text Understanding

Read the text and answer the following questions.

1) What do people understand and believe in a team work environment?

2) Why it is hard to find a place that exemplifies teamwork?

3) What are organizations working on valuing?

4) What is the traditional approach to team building for many organizations?

5) How can you put team building into every single day?

6) What is a teamwork culture?

V. Vocabulary Building

A. Match the words with their definitions.

1.	foster	a.	a place used for relaxation or recreation, attracting visitors for vacations and/or tourism
2.	collaboration	b.	a place affording peace and quiet
3.	exemplify	c.	a feeling of delight at being entertained
4.	folklore	d.	commodities offered for sale
5.	resort	e.	promote the growth of
6.	retreat	f.	act of working jointly
7.	amusement	g.	clarify by giving an example of
8.	merchandise	h.	the unwritten literature (stories and proverbs and riddles and songs) of a culture

B. Complete sentence with the words given.

foster	collaboration	exemplify	merchandise
executive	interaction	seminar	coordinate

1) The operation of an _____ team is different because employees watch the executive team closely, trying to discern the direction of the firm, particularly during tough economic periods.

2) The _____ of team members among themselves demands teamwork competence; the _____ of the executive team members with other members of the firm depends on leadership competence while the _____ of the members of the tam with persons or organizations outside the firm refers to network competence.

3) Medical, nursing, and allied health students who were rated as providing more-comprehensive care had enhanced productivity after participating in a weekly team work _____ series and practicing in two-or-three person student teams.

4) In order to _____ actions, it is important that team members understand and predict each other's behavior, and explanations can help to improve insight in other team members' behavior.

5) Fair, flexible contract can _____ cooperative relationship, so be sure the contract specifies what will happen when the scope changes, the portfolio changes, specifications change, legislative requirements change or other unknown pressures arise.

6) Leaders want to get people to think as one company. But managers in different functions or different business units seem surprisingly reluctant to work together. Jealousies, misunderstandings and enmity seem more common than _____.

7) Groups of people bring a project to closure on time. Within budget, and in alignment

with required performance standards. They _____ what great teamwork can achieve.

8) In addition to supplying replacement _____ in a timely fashion, The Limited's EPOS system can be used to monitor marketing. It can track fashion design performance, pinpointing age groups, income level, and geographic locations.

C. *Translate the following sentences into Chinese.*

1) Executive leaders communicate the clear expectation that teamwork and collaboration are expected. No one completely owns a work area or process all by himself. People who own work processes and positions are open and receptive to ideas and input from others on the team.

2) The organization members talk about and identify the value of a teamwork culture. If values are formally written and shared, teamwork is one of the key five or six.

3) Important stories and folklore that people discuss within the company emphasize teamwork. People who "do well" and are promoted within the company are team players.

4) Provide training in systematic methods so the team expends its energy on the project, not on figuring out how to work together as a team to approach it.

D. *Read the following passage about the team building process. Choose the best heading for each of the paragraphs.*

1) _____. Meet with the team leader (maybe even the full team) to determine why they think team building is necessary and what they hope to achieve. You should also clarify your role, the data collection proves, and what they can expect from team building.

2) _____. The purpose is to collect information that will help you and the team understand the issues and identify both the strengths and weaknesses of the team. Typical methods include interviews, focus groups, surveys, and observation.

3) _____. Use the data to clarify the issues faced by the team and determine both the goals and methods of the team building intervention.

4) _____. Usually a one-or-two-day meeting designed to increase the effectiveness of the team and the members. The meeting will provide feedbacks on the data collected as well as appropriate exercises, activities, surveys, discussions, and the creation of plans to improve the functioning of the team.

5) _____. There should be some method of assessing the extent to which the goals of the team were achieved. Methods may include comparing the data collected prior to the intervention with a similar data set collected at selected internals following the intervention.

    a. Data Collection
    b. Contracting
    c. Evaluation
    d. Diagnosis
    e. Team Building Intervention

VI. Further Reading

Twelve Cs for Team Building

Executives, managers and organization staff members universally explore ways to improve business results and profitability. Many view team-based, horizontal, organization structures as the best design for involving all employees in creating business success.

No matter what you call your team-based improvement effort: continuous improvement, total quality, lean manufacturing or self-directed work teams, you are striving to improve results for customers. Few organizations, however, are totally pleased with the results their team improvement efforts produce. If your team improvement efforts are not living up to your expectations, this self-diagnosing checklist may tell you why. Successful team building, that creates effective, focused work teams, requires attention to each of the following.

Clear Expectations: Has executive leadership clearly communicated its expectations for the team's performance and expected outcomes? Do team members understand why the team was created? Is the organization demonstrating constancy of purpose in supporting the team with resources of people, time and money? Does the work of the team receive sufficient emphasis as a priority in terms of the time, discussion, attention and interest directed its way by executive leaders?

Context: Do team members understand why they are participating on the team? Do they understand how the strategy of using teams will help the organization attain its communicated business goals? Can team members define their team's importance to the accomplishment of corporate goals? Does the team understand where its work fits in the total context of the organization's goals, principles, vision and values?

Commitment: Do team members want to participate on the team? Do team members feel the team mission is important? Are members committed to accomplishing the team mission and expected outcomes? Do team members perceive their service as valuable to the organization and to their own careers? Do team members anticipate recognition for their contributions? Do team members expect their skills to grow and develop on the team? Are team members excited and challenged by the team opportunity?

Competence: Does the team feel that it has the appropriate people participating? (As an example, in a process improvement, is each step of the process represented on the team?) Does the team feel that its members have the knowledge, skill and capability to address the issues for which the team was formed? If not, does the team have access to the help it needs? Does the team feel it has the resources, strategies and support needed to accomplish its mission?

Charter: Has the team taken its assigned area of responsibility and designed its own mission, vision and strategies to accomplish the mission. Has the team defined and communicated its goals; its anticipated outcomes and contributions; its timelines; and how it will measure both the outcomes of its work and the process the team followed to accomplish their task? Does the leadership team or other coordinating group support what the team has designed?

Control: Does the team have enough freedom and empowerment to feel the ownership necessary to accomplish its charter? At the same time, do team members clearly understand their boundaries? How far may members go in pursuit of solutions? Are limitations (i. e. monetary and time resources) defined at the beginning of the project before the team experiences barriers and rework? Is the team's reporting relationship and accountability understood by all members of the organization? Has the organization defined the team's authority? To make recommendations? To implement its plan? Is there a defined review process so both the team and the organization are consistently aligned in direction and purpose? Do team members hold each other accountable for project timelines, commitments and results? Does the organization have a plan to increase opportunities for self-management among organization members?

Collaboration: Does the team understand team and group process? Do members understand the stages of group development? Are team members working together effectively interpersonally? Do all team members understand the roles and responsibilities of team members? Team leaders? Team recorders? Can the team approach problem solving, process improvement, goal setting and measurement jointly? Do team members cooperate to accomplish the team charter? Has the team established group norms or rules of conduct in areas such as conflict resolution, consensus decision making and meeting management? Is the team using an appropriate strategy to accomplish its action plan?

Communication: Are team members clear about the priority of their tasks? Is there an established method for the teams to give feedback and receive honest performance feedback? Does the organization provide important business information regularly? Do the teams understand the complete context for their existence? Do team members communicate clearly and honestly with each other? Do team members bring diverse opinions to the table? Are necessary conflicts raised and addressed?

Creative Innovation: Is the organization really interested in change? Does it value creative thinking, unique solutions, and new ideas? Does it reward people who take reasonable risks to make improvements? Or does it reward the people who fit in and maintain the status quo? Does it provide the training, education, access to books and films, and field trips necessary to stimulate new thinking?

Consequences: Do team members feel responsible and accountable for team achievements? Do team members fear reprisal? Do team members spend their time finger pointing rather than resolving problems? Is the organization designing reward systems that recognize both team and individual performance? Is the organization planning to share gains and increased profitability with team and individual contributors? Can contributors see their impact on increased organization success?

Coordination: Are teams coordinated by a central leadership team that assists the groups to obtain what they need for success? Have priorities and resource allocation been planned across departments? Do teams understand the concept of the internal customer—the next process, anyone to whom they provide a product or a service? Are cross-functional and multi-department teams common and working together effectively? Is the organization developing a customer-focused process-focused orientation and moving away from traditional departmental thinking?

Cultural Change: Does the organization recognize that the team-based, collaborative, empowering, enabling organizational culture of the future is different from the traditional, hierarchical organization it may currently be? Is the organization planning to or in the process of changing how it rewards, recognizes, appraises, hires, develops, plans with, motivates and manages the people it employs? Does the organization plan to use failures for learning and support reasonable risks? Does the organization recognize that the more it can change its climate to support teams, the more it will receive in pay back from the work of the teams?

Spend time and attention on each of these twelve tips to ensure your work teams contributing most effectively to your business success. Your team members will love you, your business will soar, and empowered people will "own" and be responsible for their work processes. Can your work life get any better than this?

(1131 words)

A. *Define each of the twelve Cs in one sentence.*

✍

B. *Collocations*:

business results and profitability	address the issues
reasonable risks	clearly and honestly
self-directed	self-diagnosing

_____ work teams.

_____ checklist.

Team members communicate _____ with each other.

It rewards people who take _____ to make improvements.

Explore ways to improve _____.

Have the knowledge, skill and capability to _____ for which the team was formed.

C. *Use words you have learnt to explain the underlined words in the sentences below.*

1) If your team improvement efforts are not <u>living up to</u> your expectations, this self-

diagnosing checklist may tell you why. Successful team building, that creates effective, focused work teams, requires attention to each of the following.

2) Is the organization demonstrating <u>constancy</u> of purpose in supporting the team with resources of people, time and money?

3) Do they understand how the strategy of using teams will help the organization <u>attain</u> its communicated business goals?

4) Can team members define their team's importance to the <u>accomplishment</u> of corporate goals?

5) Do team members <u>perceive</u> their service as valuable to the organization and to their own careers?

6) Does the team have enough freedom and <u>empowerment</u> to feel the ownership necessary to accomplish its charter?

7) Is there a defined review process so both the team and the organization are <u>consistently</u> aligned in direction and purpose?

8) Do team members hold each other <u>accountable for</u> project timelines, commitments and results?

9) Does it reward the people who fit in and maintain the <u>status quo</u>?

10) Do team members fear <u>reprisal</u>?

Culture Notes

Ice breaker

An ice breaker is an activity, game, or event that is used to welcome and warm up the conversation among participants in a meeting, training class, team building session, or other events. Any event that requires people to comfortably interact with each other and a facilitator is an opportunity to use an ice breaker. An effective ice breaker will warm up the conversation in your training class or meeting, reinforce the topic of the session, and ensure that participants enjoy their interaction and the session. When participants don't know each other, the ice breaker will help them introduce themselves to the other participants.

Part Two Writing

Writing Skills: Memo Writing

I. What is a memo

- A hard-copy (sent on paper) document.
- Used for communicating inside an organization.
- Usually short.

- Contains To, From, Date, Subject Headings and Message sections.
- Does not need to be signed, but sometimes has the sender's name at the bottom to be more friendly, or the sender's full name to be more formal. If in doubt, follow your company style.

II. Why write memos

Memos are useful in situations where emails or text messages are not suitable. For example, if you are sending an object, such as a book or a paper that needs to be signed, through internal office mail, you can use a memo as a covering note to explain what the receiver should do.

III. How to write a memo

Memos should have the following sections and content:
- A "To" section containing the name of the receiver. For informal memos, the receiver's given name; e.g. "To: Andy" is enough. For more formal memos, use the receiver's full name. If the receiver is in another department, use the full name and the department name. It is usually not necessary to use Mr., Mrs., Miss or Ms unless the memo is very formal.
- A "From" section containing the name of the sender. For informal memos, the sender's other name; e.g. "From: Bill" is enough. For more formal memos, use the sender's full name. If the receiver is in another department, use the full name and the department name. It is usually not necessary to use Mr., Mrs., Miss or Ms unless the memo is very formal.
- A "Date" section. To avoid confusion between the British and American date systems, write the month as a word or an abbreviation; e.g. "January" or "Jan".
- A Subject Heading.
- The message.

Unless the memo is a brief note, a well-organized memo message should contain the following sections:
- Situation—an Introduction or the purpose of the memo.
- Problem (optional).
- Solution (optional).
- Action—this may be the same as the solution, or be a part of the solution that the receiver needs to carry out.
- Politeness—to avoid the receiver refusing to take the action you want, it is important to end with a polite expression; e.g. "Once again, thank you for your support.", or more informally "Thanks".

IV. Sample 1

> ### MEMO
>
> **To:** David Smith, Regional Manager
> **From:** Richard Lang, Sales
> **Date:** 11 April 2014
> **Subject:** Notification of My Resignation
>
> I am writing to inform you of my intention to resign from ABC Limited.
>
> I have appreciated very much my six years working for the company. The training has been excellent and I have gained valuable experience working within an efficient and professional team. In particular, I have appreciated your personal guidance during these first years of my career.
>
> I feel now that it is time to further develop my knowledge and skills base in a different environment.
>
> I would like to leave, if possible, in a month's time on Saturday, 10 May. This will allow me to complete my current workload. I hope that this suggested arrangement is acceptable to the company.
>
> Once again, thank you for your support.

V. Sample 2

> ### Memorandum
>
> To: All Employees
> From: Brian Adams
> Date: 28 April, 2014
> Subject: Fitness Center
>
> The board of directors approved the idea for a new Fitness Center at its meeting yesterday. Work on the Fitness Center will begin immediately and should be completed within 90 days. An employee representative from each division will be appointed to determine the type of equipment and programs that will be made available.
>
> We are happy to be able to provide a facility that will contribute to the physical fitness of all our employees. Your representative on the task force will contact you soon for your suggestions about activities and equipments.

VI. Exercise

Complete the following memo with the information given below.

You are Tony Wang, a supervisor of a big company. The chief of operations (David Jacks) wants to adopt the "punch-in" system to increase productivity. Write a memo to talk about this.

Part Three　Case Study

Teamwork and Collaboration across Departments

Getting teams from different parts of an organization to work together effectively often comes down to a question of having some sense of shared enterprise. This is especially true when the members of a project team are predominantly from one part of an organization, while other team members belong to parts of the organization that will see little or no direct benefit from the project. Therefore, showing clearly, early on, how the success of the project benefits the entire organization is important. The ways in which you can do that effectively vary depending on the culture of the organization within which the project is taking place. A clear and vivid articulation of the project vision and how it supports the goals of the organization is a good first step. It is also important to connect a particular project with what is happening in other parts of the organization and demonstrate how the success of the project ultimately benefits everyone. But this is just the first hurdle.

The second hurdle—and this is common to all teams, whether from the same organizational unit or a diverse group—is to turn a group of individuals into a team. There is a lot of good literature available around this second problem, covering things like the right number of members; the ways in which a team reaches decisions—consensus versus majority, for example; how roles are assigned; maintaining momentum throughout a project; and dealing with successes and failures.

A key factor in the success of such collaborations is their multidisciplinary nature. People with different backgrounds bring different perspectives to a collaboration, and their diverse inputs help a team to see things in new ways—and sometimes come up with innovative concepts.

But those different perspectives can sometimes be a source of conflict. Therefore, if you want to be able to work effectively with people in other disciplines and help ensure your product team's success, you should make a concerted effort to gain sufficient understanding of your team members' various roles and responsibilities, so you can communicate with them in their own language and respond to their needs. Reading about the other disciplines that are represented on your product team is a great way to learn about those roles and gives you the background you'll need to understand what you experience on the job. Of course, you'll learn the most by simply observing how your coworkers accomplish their work and engaging them in conversation about their work. People love to talk about what they do, so encourage your peers in other disciplines to share their work experiences with you, and listen with an open mind.

A. *Answer the following questions:*

1. What does it mean by "Getting teams from different parts of an organization to work together effectively often comes down to a question of having some sense of shared enterprise"?

2. Why is the multidisciplinary nature of the team members a key factor in the success of such collaborations?

3. How can we deal with the issues that will arise when the different perspectives can sometimes be a source of conflict?

B. *You are Team Results, a company providing help to those companies needing help. Read the need below and provide a solution.*

> **The Need:** A globally-known car maker needed its dealerships to freeze sales during a long weekend so that the system could be overhauled to meet new tax regulations. The dealerships met the request with a hostile and angry refusal. The company was facing an impasse on a national scale, complications on every side, and a non-negotiable deadline for tax compliance.

Unit Five

Initiation

Note on the topic

项目启动是指组织正式开始一个项目或继续到项目的下一个阶段。通过发布项目章程正式地启动确定这个项目。项目章程是一个非常重要的文件,该文件正式确认项目的存在并对项目提供简要的概述。主要利益相关者要在项目章程上签字,以表示承认在项目需求和目的上达成一致。同时重要的是要确认项目经理并进行授权。

项目正式开始有两个明确的标志。一是任命项目经理、建立项目管理班子;二是下达项目许可证书。项目经理的选择和核心项目组的组建是项目启动的关键环节,强有力的领导是优秀项目管理的必要组成部分。项目经理必须领导项目成员,处理好与关键项目干系人的关系,理解项目的商业需求,准备可行的项目计划。

Part One Reading

Ⅰ. Before you read

A. Discuss the following questions in a group.

1) What is your style of taking actions? Sensible one or impulsive one?

2) True or false.

An old saying goes like this "think before you leap". Do you agree? Give your reasons.

B. Skim the text and answer the following questions:

1) What is a PID?

2) In what way are PID's good practices?

3) What are in a PID?

Ⅱ. Text Reading

A Project Initiation Document

A project **initiation** document is a reference document produced at the

outset of a project. It contains a range of information **pertain**ing to the project including its background, deliverables and ownership. One of the most comforting things to have as a project manager is a full awareness of the customer's requirements, the **deliverables** and the knowledge that the project has strong foundations with both firm ownership and sound business case. Capturing and documenting key information such as this before a project kicks off is an essential activity and a project initiation document or PID provides a place to store it.

Project initiation documents are nothing new and are parts of many formal project methodologies. Too often when projects have problems, attempting to understand what's going wrong and why can be difficult. In a poor project environment—things often go undocumented—trying to **unravel** something that was agreed in conversation can be **fraught**. PID's are good practice as they capture key information that can be used for reference throughout a project for guidance or when clarification is required. They also provide a method of communicating the benefits and business cases that prove a project should be **commenced** in the first place.

Producing the PID at the right time is essential—the PID should be produced while the Project is being started. It can be authored by a mix of the customer and the project manager and should ultimately summarize your project in one document. As projects can be big/small, simple/complicated the actual construction of PID's may vary from project to project but there are some fundamentals that you should consider including in your PID.

What's in a Project Initiation Document

The contents of a PID may vary from project to project—there are however some key elements:

Project Goals: Layout in simple terms the goals of the project—this should include reference to the **rationale** behind the goal—for example—a project goal could be to reduce the risk of legacy technology by introducing a new ERP system. Notice there is a difference between Goals or Objectives and Deliverables.

Deliverables: What will the project deliver? —for example is the project to deliver a written report, is it delivering a new IT system, is it delivering training—there may be multiple deliverables that need to be documented—ensure that the deliverables are measurable, so it can be proved beyond reasonable doubt that tasks have been completed.

Scope: What is the scope of the project—for example is the scope "implement IT solution for Australian user base". Note this should clearly explain whom the project will be done to and anything that is excluded.

Financial Business Case: The business case should contain details of the expected costs of the project. The business case should also indicate any savings that may result from the project—some business cases take a multi-year approach (e.g. 5 years) looking at the long term impact of the financial commitment.

Project Roles and Responsibilities: A clear part of the PID is clearly outlining the authorities within a project. The PID should outline the project structure e. g. sponsor, steering team, project manager, project team and their levels of responsibilities—you may even consider drawing up job descriptions for the people within the team. The PID should define the resource requirement for running the project—for example does the project require a team of 10? If it does explain why.

Risks: Consider any risks that may affect the project—their likelihood of their occurrence and their possible impact, including **mitigation** against the risks that you've identified.

Assumptions/Constraints: Are there any assumptions or constraints that you need to make about the project? For example, an assumption of introducing a new IT system may make some assumptions about what applications the system may integrate with.

Project Controls: Project controls, help schedule and measure projects—think about whether the project requires key performance indicators.

Reporting Framework: Consider what information channels will be required during the project—will a monthly summary report to the project sponsor **suffice**? Or will it need something else?

PID Sign Off: At sign off it is important to assess the PID and ask if it adequately represents the project — is possible ensure that the customer of the project signs the document as a part of its release.

Constructing a thorough project initiation document is a key part of starting a project. Ensuring that key elements of a project, such as its goals and business case, well understood is imperative. A PID can be referenced throughout a project and serves as a valuable route map for the project team. Whilst their contents may vary getting down what's important to your project can be a really valuable activity.

(788 words)

Ⅲ. Words to Note

initiation	n.	启动,开始
outset	n.	开端
pertain	v.	与某事物有关联
deliverable	n.	交付物
unravel	v.	(使某事物)变清楚或获解决
fraught	a.	担心的;烦恼的;焦虑的;令人忧虑的
commence	v.	开始
rationale	n.	基本原理;理论基础
mitigation	n.	减轻,缓和
suffice	v.	能满足(某人,某事物)之需要的

IV. Text Understanding

Read the text and answer the following questions.

1) What is the essential activity before a project kick off?

2) What can the key information captured by the PID used for?

3) What are the key elements that a PID may include?

4) What should the business case contain?

5) How do the Project Controls work?

6) What is a key part of starting a project?

V. Vocabulary Building

A. *Match the words with their definitions.*

initiation	a.	start (*n.*)
outset	b.	worried or anxious; worrying
pertain	c.	start (*v.*)
deliverable	d.	fundamental reason for or logical basis of something
unravel	e.	reduction in the unpleasantness, seriousness, or painfulness of something
fraught	f.	beginning
commence	g.	be connected with or relevant to something
rationale	h.	something that a company has promised to have ready for a customer, especially parts of computer systems
mitigation	i.	(cause something to) become clear or solved
suffice	j.	be enough (for someone/something); be adequate

B. *Complete sentence with the words given.*

fraught	rationale	mitigation	suffice
initiation	outset	pertain	deliverable

1) The outsourcing "life cycle" is the series of stages that an agreement/contract goes through from its _____ to steady state operation.

2) Managing any procurement has its challenges. However, with failing public sector IT outsourcing projects frequently reported by the media, we believe that the development of a robust procurement strategy at the _____ of any outsourcing project will be vital to its ultimate success.

3) One of the most fascinating aspect of the outsourcing results _____ to where will the outsourcing growth come from in the future.

4) Given the increase in global IT outsourcing agreements, many companies will be looking at outsourcing QA and testing as an independent validation and acceptance phase in order to ensure high quality _____ and gain competitive advantages.

5) Outsourcing can offer definite advantages—but only if you do it right. Outsourcing is _____ with danger for the unwary executive or corporate counsel.

6) In this article, I want to look a little more closely at the _____ behind outsourcing IT services and making sound outsourcing decisions. The trick is to balance the possible benefits, such as streamlining processes and reducing costs, with the associated risks involved in weakening your competitive advantages by outsourcing a critical component of the business.

7) Outsourcing is a strategic, highly successful business tool for positive organizational changes. Nonetheless, managing outsourcing relationships can be a complex process. It is important for an organization to be aware of what drives outsourcing success and the framework that covers risk identification and _____ strategy.

8) Must the terms and conditions for clients declare anonymized data processing abroad or does it _____ to indicate that data processing is outsourced to a third party?

C. Translate the following sentences into Chinese.

1) A project initiation document is a reference document produced at the outset of a project. It contains a range of information pertaining to the project including its background, deliverables and ownership. One of the most comforting things to have as a project manager is a full awareness of the customer's requirements, the deliverables and the knowledge that the project has strong foundations with both firm ownership and sound business case. The organization members talk about and identify the value of a teamwork culture. If values are formally written and shared, teamwork is one of the key five or six.

2) Producing the PID at the right time is essential—the PID should be produced while the Project is being started. It can be authored by a mix of the customer and the project manager and should ultimately summarize your project in one document.

3) Constructing a thorough project initiation document is a key part of starting a project. Ensuring that key elements of a project, such as its goals and business case, are well understood is imperative.

D. Read the following passage about the SLAs. Choose the best heading for each of the paragraphs.

The Service Level Agreements (SLAs) should detail the minimum level of service to be provided by the outsourcing vendor. They should be objective and measurable and have no ambiguity. This helps both parties in the long term. Some good examples of the type of SLAs that should be considered are:

1) _____—dates must be agreed from the outset on all major deliverables with all efforts to ensure they are met. Use change control processes if these dates need to be moved.

2) _____—periodic surveys should be conducted to make sure that the service provided by the outsourcing company is satisfactory to customers.

3) _____—effectiveness metrics focus on lowering costs, improving profit, and adjusting business transactions.

4) _____—the volume of work sometimes is difficult to define. For example, projects that are billed on a time-and-material basis may discuss volume in terms of number of resources, while a fixed-price project usually specifies number of deliverables. This metric is an important part of the SLA.

5) _____—sensitivity metrics measure the amount of time required for an outsource company to handle a request.

6) _____—in outsourcing, guaranteeing 100% availability of services costs significantly more than guaranteeing 99% or 98%, and not every company or every application needs 100% reliability. The SLA should request service availability to meet specific business needs.

It is also good to ensure that SLAs are tied into the contract, sometimes on a risk/reward basis to ensure that there is mutual interest in meeting them.

a. Volume of Work
b. Sensitivity
c. System Downtime and Availability
d. On time delivery
e. Client Satisfaction
f. Effectiveness

VI. Further Reading

Writing an Outsourcing Contract

It is hard to over-emphasize how important the content of an outsourcing contract is. Once you have an outsourcing contract in place, the clauses of this agreement will guide your outsourcer's every move, and may act to free you to do business or <u>feel like a straitjacket</u>. Here, in layman's terms, are some points to consider when planning the contract. Be sure to use an attorney who is familiar with and has experience writing outsourcing agreements.

Example contracts are hard to come by, because each one is so closely <u>tailored to</u> the particular case, and often has a confidentiality clause that makes the contract itself proprietary information.

An outsourcing agreement is much like any other contract: it is putting in writing what the two companies agree will be done by each party, and usually how it will be paid for. If you have worked with government contracts, you may see numerous similarities. Typical contracts contain the following parts:

- Scope of Work.
- Deliverables.
- Terms and Conditions.
- Service Level Agreement.

1. Scope of Work

The Scope of Work explains what the outsourcing firm will do for the clients. In an Information Technology outsourcing arrangement, for example, it may describe how the outsourcer will build a computer system to do some task, test it to prescribed criteria, and turn it over to operations (at which point the Service Level Agreement takes over).

It is very important to cover every aspect of the system that you possibly can think of. The outsourcer will base their price on the content of this section, so if you leave something out, they will quite legitimately want more funding to add it in later.

Where applicable, you might want to include such detail as:

- Equipment they must procure and/or maintain, including type and serial number, if existing.
- Software they must procure and/or maintain, including module names and versions, if existing.
- Telecommunications circuits, including number and line speed.
- Data backup and archiving activities.
- Functional specifications they must implement.
- Work Plan. Ask the outsourcer to provide a detailed plan of how they intend to accomplish the work. Once you agree that it is reasonable, make it part of the contract. It should include specifics: what will be accomplished by when. (If dates cannot be used because you can't accurately forecast the project's begin date, get them to specify accomplishments in terms of how many days each item will be done after the start date of the contract).

What's "**in scope**" and "**out of scope**" will be discussed *daily* once the contract is in force. Make sure it covers your needs.

2. Deliverables

List everything that the outsourcer is supposed to provide, install, and/or turn over, to the client, in as much detail as possible. Include everything, even if the items remain on the contractor's books (i.e., for tax advantages). List a due date when possible, and cover the equipment's entire life cycle through lawful disposal. Where documentation is included, consider the following:

- Multiple copies, with accessible backup maintained by outsourcer.
- Drawings in a data format your computer can read. (i.e., if contractor did their work on Intergraph CAD equipment and you have only AutoCAD, demand AutoCAD files of the as-built drawings!)
- Documentation must conform to industry standards.
- Detailed schematic of the network, including locations, user area contacts, TCP/IP addresses, serial numbers, and phone numbers.

3. Terms and Conditions

Terms and Conditions cover the numerous details of the legalistic part of the agreement. This list mentions some key items covered in Terms and Conditions. Be sure to work with an attorney experienced in outsourcing contracts when finalizing your agreement. Deciding how you wish to treat these items is a vital step to getting your contract finalized.

- **Length** of contract: Long contracts (e.g., 10 years) have been in vogue, supposedly because they allow a client to lock in costs for a long period, but shorter contracts (3 to 5 years) provide flexibility to change outsourcers without the pain and expense of termination, and also keep the outsourcer on their toes to earn renewal business.
- **Ownership of assets, data, network**: Who will own the assets? Get help from your financial department on this, because it can have big profit and tax implications. Even if the client transfers ownership of items to the outsourcer, the client needs to retain certain control to avoid being held hostage for high costs in case of changes or termination. The outsourcer may want to have considerable control of certain assets (e.g., the network cabling) to guarantee satisfactory operations.
- **Payment terms**: They are the best if tied in with tangible, measurable results like milestones. They may also be adjustable for performance or changing processing loads, with incentives or penalties based on early or late achievement, and/or better or worse customer satisfaction measurements.
- **Risk - sharing, partnering**: In a true partnership, the client and outsourcer will share risk and reward. If the venture works well and profits are up, both benefit; if business conditions become really sour, both will suffer. These need to be balanced, remembering that you may be signing up for risk in an area you have no control.
- **Transition plan**: how will business be turned over to the outsourcer? This is a key item if personnel are involved.

You can see the possible complexity of a large outsourcing contract and this list is by no means all-inclusive. This complexity virtually guarantees that there will be changes to the contract. Put in place a mechanism for managing and emplacing these changes with a budget to avoid lost opportunity costs due to inflexibility.

4. Service Level Agreement

The Service Level Agreement, or SLA, lists the services which will be supplied on a regular basis, and includes volumes, response times, and quantitative/qualitative descriptions of these. This may be tied in with payment terms (i.e., more payment for heavier processing loads, more help desk calls, volume of training provided, more data transferred, more transactions processed, more equipment installed, greater user satisfaction as measured by survey, etc., and conversely, less for less).

(998 Words)

A. *Give brief answers to the questions below.*

1) What do typical contracts include?

2) What are the key items of the terms and conditions of a contract?

B. *Collocations*:

ongoing	interpretations
be familiar with and have experience	intimidating
complexity	inevitable
confidentiality	all-inclusive

1) _____ writing outsourcing agreements.

2) Have a _____ clause that makes the contract itself proprietary information.

3) Due to differing _____ of the text.

4) Provide an _____ operation for the client.

5) Write a contract for outsourcing services can be an _____ prospect.

6) How to agreeably handle the _____ changes and unanticipated issues/requirements.

7) A hybrid approach combines advantages of both, but at the expense of added _____.

8) This list is by no means _____.

C. *Use words you have learnt to explain the underlined words in the sentences below.*

1) Once you have an outsourcing contract in place, the clauses of this agreement will guide your outsourcer's every move, and may act to free you to do business or <u>feel like a straitjacket</u>.

2) Example contracts are hard to come by, because each one is so closely <u>tailored to</u> the particular case, and often has a confidentiality clause that makes the contract itself proprietary information.

3) The terms and conditions often will be the <u>bulkiest</u> part of the contract, because they cover so many things that may seldom or never occur, such as early termination.

4) Each contract type has <u>pros and cons</u>.

5) Be sure to work with an attorney experienced in outsourcing contracts when <u>finalizing</u> your agreement.

6) ...and also keep the outsourcer on their toes to earn renewal business.

7) Even if the client transfers ownership of items to the outsourcer, the client needs to retain certain control to avoid being held hostage for high costs in case of changes or termination.

8) Best if tied in with tangible, measurable results like milestones.

Culture Notes

Legacy technology (system).
In computing a legacy system is an old method, technology, computer system, or application program of, relating to, or being a previous or outdated computer system. A more recent definition says that "a legacy system is any corporate computer system that isn't Internet-dependent."

ERP system.
Enterprise Resource Planning (ERP) is a business management software—usually a suite of integrated applications—that a company can use to collect, store, manage and interpret data from many business activities, including product planning, cost and development, manufacturing or service delivery, marketing and sales, inventory management, and shipping and payment. ERP provides an integrated view of core business processes, often in real-time, using common databases maintained by a database management system.

Part Two   Writing

Writing Skills: Sending Contract

I. What is a business contract

Business contracts are crucial to the relationships between companies and business partners. Contracts specify the terms of agreements, services or products to be exchanged and any deadlines associated with the partnership. Business contracts prevent disputes and misunderstandings.

II. Writing Tips

1) **Label the document.** Use the terms "Contract" or "Agreement" to distinguish your contract from other legal documents in your files.

2) **Separate the document parts into segments that identify each paragraph's purpose or intent.** Label these segments with numbers or letters to clarify them from one another.

3) **List the parties involved in the contract.** Include contact information as you list the parties. As you refer to the parties later in the contract, you can shorten their identification

or names.

4) **Write out the purpose of the contract prior to providing the details.** The purpose includes the services provided, the product created, labor exerted or any other focus that pertains to the purpose of the agreement.

5) **Indicate any monetary issues.** These may include costs, payment arrangements, or interest charges for late or deferred payments. Due dates and amounts should be addressed with specific information. For instance, if a payment is due in the middle of the month, the contract should say by the 15th of the month.

6) **Identify all deadlines associated with the contract, along with the contract enactment date.** Project completion, product delivery or other timelines should be clearly written out for the protection of all parties within the contract.

7) **Explain the expiration date, along with any renewal terms, if applicable.** Many contracts expire, such as lease agreements. The details of the expiration should be explained in detail.

8) **Write into the contract any consequences for breach of contract for both parties.** Consequences often include payment for services not rendered, reimbursement for damages and automatic termination of the contract. Include details about all consequences and what breach of contract might entail.

9) **Include a confidentiality clause if any part of the partnership should be kept private.** Many transactions should not be open to the public. A confidentiality clause prevents either party from sharing details about the contract and business partnership.

10) **Provide termination conditions.** Most contracts can be terminated through modifications or other requests. Write specifics about the details surrounding how the contract may be terminated and any consequences that might result from termination.

11) **Create signature lines for all parties of the contract.** Provide spaces for printed names and dates, along with an area for a witness signature. Require that all parties sign the contract before it can be enacted.

Ⅲ. Sample Contract

This Partnership Agreement is entered into on January 1, 2014 between Jane A. Jones and Diane B. Doe, herein referred to as Partners, who will work together in accordance with the terms and conditions set forth in this document.
1) The Partnership will be known as Super Trendy Gear "N" Stuff, and the head office and principal place of business will be located at 2000 Main Street, Anytown, NJ, 10000.
2) The Partnership has been formed in order to design, manufacture, and sell casual, active clothing to the teenage female demographic.
3) The Partnership will be in effect starting January 1, 2014 and will remain in full effect unless and/or until it is dissolved by the mutual written agreement of the partners.
4) The stated and verified initial capital contribution of the partners are as follows: Jane A. Jones contributed $20 000; Diane B. Doe contributed $20 000.

a. Each partner is required to deposit her initial contribution to the partnership at the Friendly Business Bank, 1 Blank Street, Anytown, NJ, 10 000 on or before 12/29/2013.
b. Neither partner will be entitled to withdraw her initial contribution from the capital of the Partnership, without the written formal consent of the other.
c. Neither partner is entitled to claim any interest earned on these contributions as their own.
5) Any and all profits and losses will be divided equally between the partners.
6) Each partner has a contractual duty to devote the appropriate time and attention needed to promote the interests of the Partnership.
7) The partners will maintain a proper book of accounts at their main office. An accurate account of the profits, losses, assets and expenditures are to be entered in these books.
8) The fiscal year for the Partnership shall end on the 31st day of December.
9) The partners shall meet on a monthly basis to discuss any and all matters related to the management of the business. Each partner has equal rights and responsibilities.
10) A new partner may be admitted to the Partnership with the written formal consent of all other partners.
11) If so desired, the partners may reach a mutual agreement to terminate the Partnership. In this instance, the assets of the Partnership business would be sold to pay off the liabilities and obligations of the business and any balance remaining divided equally between partners.

This agreement shall be governed in accordance with the laws of the state of New Jersey. This agreement can only be amended or changed with the mutual written consent of all the partners.

IN WITNESS WHEREOF, the parties have executed this agreement on this 10th day of November, 2013 in Anytown, NJ 10 000.

Jane A. Jones

Jane A. Jones
16 W. 4th St.
Anytown, NJ 10 000

Diane B. Doe

Diane B. Doe
7967 Piedmont Cir.
Anytown, NJ 10 000

Ⅳ. Exercise

The following is a contract template with some information missing. Please study the sample contract above and the template. Choose the information from the above sample to complete the template.

This contract is entered into and between _____ [name of the First Party] and _____ [name of the Second Party].

The term of this Agreement will become effective on _____ [starting date] and shall continue until _____ [date of contract termination, if applicable].

The specific terms of this Agreement are as follows:

1) _____ [Insert details of first term].
2) _____ [Insert details of second term].
3) _____ [Insert details of third term].
4) _____ [Insert details of fourth term].

In consideration of the agreement detailed above, the First Party agrees that it shall _____ [describe the specific duties the First Party is responsible for performing].

In consideration of the agreement detailed above, the Second Party agrees that it shall _____ [describe the specific duties the Second Party is responsible for performing].

This contract cannot be modified in any way unless such modifications are made in writing and signed by both Parties. This document constitutes the entire agreement between the Parties. This Contract is legally binding upon the Parties, their successors, and heirs, and will be enforced according to the laws of _____ [appropriate governing jurisdiction: state, county, etc.].

It is agreed. By signing below, the Parties agree to be bound by the terms of this Agreement.

_____ [Signature of First Party]
_____ [Name of First Party]
_____ [Street Address]
_____ [City, State Zip Code]

_____ [Signature of Second Party]
_____ [Name of Second Party]
_____ [Street Address]
_____ [City, State Zip Code]

Date: _____, 20 _____

Part Three Case Study

Project Initiation Documents Get Your Project Off to a Great Start

Have you ever been a part of a project where not everyone has the same view of where the project is heading? This lack of clarity can breed confusion: People start pulling in different directions, building up unrealistic expectations, and harboring unnecessary worries and fears. While it's normal as part of a project to put the detailed plans, controls and reporting mechanisms into place, how do you get everyone on the same page to start with? This is accomplished by creating a Project Initiation Document (PID)—the top-level project planning document. In it, you bring together all of the information needed to get your project started, and communicate that key information to the project's stakeholders. With a well-put-together Project Initiation Document, you can let everyone understand where the project's heading from the outset.

Your Project Initiation Document does the following:
- Defines your project and its scope.
- Justifies your project.
- Secures funding for the project, if necessary.
- Defines the roles and responsibilities of project participants.
- Gives people the information they need to be productive and effective right from the start.

By creating a PID, you'll answer the questions: What? Why? Who? How? When?

Section 1: What?

This section tells the reader what the project is seeking to achieve. In it, describe the problem that the project is seeking to solve, as well as a full definition of the project. This section will typically cover the following topics.

Background: What is the context of the project, and why is the work needed? Briefly describe the idea or problem, and discuss why this project is relevant and timely. The details will come later, so use this section to highlight briefly how this project came to be.

Project Definition:
- Purpose. Why are you doing this work? Describe the desired end result of this project.
- Objectives. What specific outcomes will be achieved, and how will you measure these outcomes? Remember to limit the number of objectives for your project—four or five goals are typically enough.
- Scope. What are the boundaries for this project (for example, type of work, type of client, type of problem, geographic area covered)? List any areas excluded that you believe stakeholders might assume are included, but are not. The more specific you

are, the less opportunity there is for misunderstanding at a later stage in the project.
- Deliverables. What will the project deliver as outputs? Where you can, describe deliverables as tangible items like reports, products, or services. Remember to include a date that each deliverable is expected. You'll use this information to monitor milestones.
- Constraints: What things must you take into consideration that will influence your deliverables and schedule? These are external variables that you cannot control but need to manage.
- Assumptions: What assumptions are you making at the start of the project? If necessary, schedule work to confirm these assumptions.

Section 2: Why?

Build a business case to show why your project is going ahead. Describe the effect the project will have on the business, and support this with a detailed account of the risks that should be considered.

Business Case:
- Benefits. Why are you carrying out this project, and what benefits do you expect it to deliver? Include information on how these benefits will be measured. For more on benefits management, click here.
- Options. What other courses of action were considered as this project was designed and developed?
- Cost and Timescale. Provide a breakdown of project costs and related financing.
- Cost/Benefit Analysis. How are the costs of the project balanced against the expected returns? For details of how to construct a cost/benefit analysis, click here.

Risk Analysis:
- Risk Identification. Identify the risks within the project, and that you'll either need to manage or accept.
- Risk Prevention. Describe what you are going to do to mitigate or manage risks.
- Risk Management. Where you can't prevent risks, what are your contingency plans for dealing with them? What actions will you take should the risk materialize?
- Risk Monitoring: What processes do you have in place to routinely assess the risks associated with your project?

Section 3: Who?

Describe how the project will be organized and managed. Identify reporting lines, and outline specific roles that will be filled. You need to be clear about staff roles so that you don't duplicate responsibilities, and so that everyone is clear about what's expected of them. If this is a long-term project, you may even consider developing job descriptions for team members.

Roles and Responsibilities:
- Project Organization Chart/Structure. Create a diagram that shows the lines of authority

and reports for each project team member.
- Project Sponsor. Who has the ultimate authority and control over the project and its implementation?
- Project Manager. Who is the Project Manager, and what are his or her responsibilities?
- Project Team. Who are the key members of the project team? What are their roles and job descriptions? What are their phone numbers and email addresses? What is their original department or organization? And to whom do they report to on a daily basis?

Section 4: How and When?

Provide broad information about how the project will be implemented. Outline how the project will roll out by defining timelines, resources, and management stages. This is a high-level overview that will, as the project proceeds, be supported by more detailed project planning documents.

Initial Project Plan:
- Assignments. What major tasks (with milestones) will be completed during the project?
- Schedule. Provide a report of the estimated time involved for the project. You've probably already prepared a high level Gantt chart or similar schedule, so the PID simply summarizes the anticipated schedule.
- Human Resources. How many days activity will be needed to complete the project? How many support staff will be needed? Will you need to bring more people onto the project team?
- Project Control. How will progress be monitored and communicated?
- Quality Control. How will the quality of deliverables be evaluated and monitored?

A. *Answer the following questions:*

1) Why is the PID important to guarantee the success of a project?
2) What needs to be covered in a PID?

B.

A project initiation plan is a series of documents in project management used to control project planning, implementation and review. Each business uses its own methods and documents when creating a project initiation plan. The goals of this plan are to develop a timeline that delivers a finished product for the client, meets client expectations and remains within the budget assigned by the project management team. Identifying project goals is an indispensable component of this plan. What do you think identifying project goal needs to involve?

Unit Six

Design

Note on the topic

设计是指设计师有目标有计划地进行技术性的创作活动。设计的任务不只是为生活和商业服务,同时也伴有艺术性的创作。

根据工业设计师 Victor Papanek 的定义,设计(Design)是为构建有意义的秩序而付出的有意识的直觉上的努力。第一步,理解用户的期望、需要、动机,并理解业务、技术和行业上的需求和限制。第二步,将这些所知道的东西转化为对产品的规划(或者产品本身),使得产品的形式、内容和行为变得有用、能用、令人向往,并且在经济和技术上可行。这是设计的意义和基本要求所在。

设计管理就是:"根据使用者的需求,有计划有组织地进行研究与开发管理活动。有效地积极调动设计师的开发创造性思维,把市场与消费者的认识转换在新产品中,以新的更合理、更科学的方式影响和改变人们的生活,并为企业获得最大限度的利润而进行的一系列设计策略与设计活动的管理。"

Part One　Reading

I. Before you read

A. *Answer the following questions.*

1) Describe one of your experiences of designing a plan in order to achieve something.

2) What are the things that you take into consideration when you design your plan?

3) True or false.

An old Chinese saying goes like this, "预则立,不预则废". While in English it goes like this, "Any success depends upon previous preparations." Do you agree? Give your reasons.

B. *Skim the text and answer the following questions*:

1) What are goals and objectives?

2) In what ways are goals and objectives different?

II. Text Reading

Defining Project Goals and Objectives

1. Goals and Objectives

Goals and objectives are statements that describe what the project will accomplish, or the business value the project will achieve.

Goals are high level statements that provide overall context for what the project is trying to achieve, and should **align** to business goals.

Objectives are lower level statements that describe the specific, **tangible** products and deliverables that the project will deliver.

The definition of goals and objectives is more of an art than a science, and it can be difficult to define them and align them correctly.

2. Goals

Goals are high-level statements that provide the overall context for what the project is trying to accomplish. Let's look at an example and some of the characteristics of a goal statement. One of the goals of a project might be to "increase the overall satisfaction levels for clients calling to the company helpdesk with support needs".

Because the goal is at a high-level, it may take more than one project to achieve. In the above example, for instance, there may be a technology component to increase clients' satisfaction. There may also be new procedures, new training classes, reorganization of the helpdesk department and **modification** of the company rewards system. It may take many projects over a long period of time to achieve the goal.

The goal should refer the business benefit in terms of cost, speed and / or quality. In this example, the focus is on quality of service. Even if the project is not directly in support of the business, there should be an indirect tie. For instance, an IT infrastructure project to install new web servers may ultimately allow faster client response, better price performance, or other business benefit. If there is no business value to the project, the project should not be started.

Generally, non-measurable: If you can measure the achievement of your goal, it is probably at too low a level and is probably more of an objective.

If your goal is not achievable through any combination of projects, it is probably written at too high a level. In the above example, you could **envision** one or more projects that could end up achieving a higher level of client satisfaction. A goal statement that says you are trying to achieve a perfect client experience is not possible with any combination of projects. It may instead be a vision statement, which is a higher level statement showing direction and **aspiration**, but which may never actually be achieved.

It is important to understand business and project goal statements, even though goals are not a part of the TenStep Project Definition. Goals are most important from a business perspective. The project manager needs to understand the business goals that the project is trying to contribute to. However, you do not need to define specific project goals. On the other hand, objectives are definitely important.

3. Objectives

Objectives are concrete statements describing what the project is trying to achieve. The objective should be written at a lower level, so that it can be evaluated at the conclusion of a project to see whether it was achieved or not. Goal statements are designed to be vague. Objectives should not be vague. A well-worded objective will be Specific, Measurable, Attainable/Achievable, Realistic and Time-bound (SMART).

An example of an objective statement might be to "upgrade the helpdesk telephone system by December 31 to achieve average client waiting times of no more than two minutes".

Note that the objective is much more concrete and specific than the goal statement.

The objective is measurable in terms of the average client waiting times the new phone system is trying to achieve.

We must assume that the objective is achievable and realistic.

The objective is time-bound, and should be completed by December 31.

Objectives should refer to the deliverables of the project. In this case, it refers to the upgrade of the telephone system. If you cannot determine what deliverables are being created to achieve the objective, then the objective may be written at too high a level. On the other hand, if an objective describes the characteristics of the deliverables, they are written at too low a level. If they describe the features and functions, they are requirements, not objectives.

(710 words)

III. Words to Note

align	v.	支持
tangible	a.	有形的
modification	n.	修改
envision	v.	预想,想象
aspiration	n.	渴望

IV. Text Understanding

Read the text and answer the following questions.

1) In what way are goals and objectives different?

2) How can a goal reference a business benefit?

3) Why sometimes a project should not be started?

4) What goals may be at too low a level?

5) Why an objective should be written at a lower level?

6) What is a well-worded objective?

V. Vocabulary Building

A. *Match the words with their definitions.*

1.	align	a.	Partial alteration
2.	tangible	b.	to picture mentally, especially some future event or events
3.	modification	c.	a goal or objective desired
4.	envision	d.	give support to
5.	aspiration	e.	(of an asset) having actual physical existence, and therefore capable of being assigned a value in monetary terms

B. *Complete sentence with the words given.*

| align   tangible   upgrade   envision   aspiration   modification |

1) The organization uses a business profile which is a production function that expresses for each business unit type the number of service units needed for all the involved service activities. Furthermore, the client organization then has to _____ its service activities with its outsourced technological activities using a service profile.

2) Selling services is significantly different than selling a _____ product. When a customer or prospect can see and feel a product, they tend to have significantly fewer questions as compared to the number of questions they have when considering purchasing something that is not _____. This means that your sales skills will need to be a consistently higher level of polish in order to be successful in selling outsourcing services.

3) Not surprisingly, the response from the established legal community was formidable and the pushback was fierce. In an effort to quell an anticipated rebellious outrage, the ABA established a follow up ABA Commission on Ethics 20/20 to undertake a thorough review of the ABA Model Rules of Professional Conduct to determine where and to what extent they required _____ to conform to the imperative of outsourcing.

4) Given the large volume of images and the limited training and expertise needed to perform this task, we _____ outsourcing this work to a global community of online cloud identifiers (CIs). However, little is known about the productivity and quality of work that can be expected from such an arrangement.

5) Our aim is always to work with each customer, not just for them, supporting their professional and personal _____ over the long-term.

6) Today, as information technology grows rapidly, new technologies reduce service and maintenance costs. At the same time, however, _____ and migrating company information systems produce such problems as high _____ costs, high complexity, and _____ and migration risks.

C. Translate the following sentences into Chinese.

1) Goals and objectives are statements that describe what the project will accomplish, or the business value the project will achieve.

2) There may also be new procedures, new training classes, reorganization of the helpdesk department and modification of the company rewards system. It may take many projects over a long period of time to achieve the goal.

3) Objectives are concrete statements describing what the project is trying to achieve. The objective should be written at a lower level, so that it can be evaluated at the conclusion of a project to see whether it was achieved or not. Goal statements are designed to be vague. Objectives should not be vague. A well-worded objective will be Specific, Measurable, Attainable/Achievable, Realistic and Time-bound (SMART).

D. Read the following passage about "Designing a Good Project". Choose the best heading for each part.

A project is a structure developed to produce a specifically defined deliverable or set of deliverables. It is time bound with specific objectives and specific resources assigned to it. Designing a project is a creative activity. You are making something that did not exist before.

1. _____

Project design is an art because you use your imagination to help others live better lives, Science is the logic used to realize those imaginations.

2. _____

A project design becomes a much easier and enjoyable experience if done in a team environment. A team of 3~5 becomes a pretty robust team for project design. It becomes all the more enjoyable and creative if the team is a set of heterogeneous individuals. In the field of agricultural research it has been found that a team or a consortium with a heterogeneous mix of various disciplines, ages and backgrounds working towards a common goal yields the most successful (most likely to be funded as well) projects of all.

3. _____

Accept it. A project design takes time. Designing a simple and small project itself will take 50 ~ 150 hours of quality time spreading over several months. Complex projects involving multiple partners will take a lot more time. Some of the common time consumers apart from thinking and writing are waiting for approvals, comments from partners and donors.

4. _____

You should not expect all proposals to be funded.

5. _____

Almost all research projects involve collaboration among different stakeholders and colleague groups. Below are some points that will emphasis why partners are important,

- Donors like investors prefer to share and spread risks.
- Donors are more inclined towards projects that include domestic institutions.
- Donors like to fund as many grantees as possible, so more partners the merrier.

6. _____

While reviewing proposals donors look for projects that adopt an integrated approach that involves all the key participants and is thus likely to contribute to significant impacts in the shortest possible time.

7. _____

There are lots of difficulties in assessing the impact of a project. Questions like how long will the benefits last, or who will take the credit proping up quite often. You and your organization need to think about impact assessment. You need to measure impacts and demonstrate impacts in your projects in order to attract donors.

8. _____

And last but not the least, you need to know the art of selling your project, so project proposal should have it in them that will answer the donor's question "What is in it for me?"

  a. Partners are important.

  b. Recognize the trends towards holistic.

  c. Project Design—Art or Science?

  d. Good Project Design is a result of team work.

  e. Project Design takes time.

  f. Be prepared for failures.

  g. Demonstrating impact is essential.

  h. Packaging is what it is all about.

VI. Further Reading

Engineering Design Process

The **engineering design process** is the formulation of a plan to help an engineer build a product with a specified performance goal. This process involves a number of steps, and parts of the process may need to be repeated many times before production of a final product can begin.

Engineering design is the process of devising a system, component, or process to meet desired needs. It is a decision-making process (often interative), in which the basic science and mathematics and engineering sciences are applied to convert resources optimally to meet a stated objective. Among the fundamental elements of the design process are the establishment of objectives and criteria, synthesis, analysis, construction, testing and evaluation. The engineering design component of a curriculum must include most of the following features: development of student creativity, use of open-ended problems, development and use of modern design theory and methodology, formulation of design problem statements and specification, consideration of alternative solutions, feasibility considerations, production processes, concurrent engineering design, and detailed system description. Further it is essential to include a variety of realistic constraints, such as economic factors, safety, reliability, aesthetics, ethics and social impact.

—**ABET Definition of Design**

The engineering design process is a <u>multi-step</u> process including the research, conceptualization, feasibility assessment, establishing design requirements, preliminary design, detailed design, production planning and tool design, and finally production. The sections to follow are not necessary steps in the engineering design process, for some tasks are completed at the same time as other tasks. This is just a general summary of each part of the engineering design process.

1. Research

A significant amount of time is spent on researching, or locating information. Consideration should be given to the existing <u>applicable</u> literature, problems and successes associated with existing solutions, costs, and marketplace needs.

The source of information should be relevant, including existing solutions. Reverse engineering can be an effective technique if other solutions are available on the market. Other sources of information include the Internet, local libraries, available government documents, personal organizations, trade journals, vendor catalogs, etc.

2. Conceptualization

Once an engineering issue is defined, solutions must be identified. These solutions can be found by using ideation, or the mental process by which ideas are generated. The following are the most widely used techniques:

- **Trigger word**—a word or phrase associated with the issue at hand is stated, and subsequent words and phrases are evoked. For example, to *move* something from one place to another may evoke *run*, *swim*, *roll*, etc.
- **Morphological chart**—independent design characteristics are listed in a chart, and different engineering solutions are proposed for each solution. Normally, a preliminary

sketch and short report accompany the morphological chart.
- **Synthesis**—the engineer imagines him or herself as the item and asks, "What would I do if I were the system?" This unconventional method of thinking may find a solution to the problem at hand. The vital aspect of the conceptualization step is synthesis. Synthesis is the process of taking the element of the concept and arranging them in the proper way. Synthesis is a creative process and is present in every design.
- **Brainstorming**—this popular method involves thinking of different ideas and adopting these ideas in some form as a solution to the problem.

3. Feasibility assessment

The purpose of a feasibility assessment is to determine whether the engineer's project can proceed into the design phase. This is based on two criterias: the project needs to be based on an achievable idea, and it needs to be within cost constraints. It is important to have an engineer with experience and good judgment to be involved in this portion of the feasibility study.

4. Establishing the design requirements

Establishing design requirements is one of the most important elements in the design process, and this task is normally performed at the same time as the feasibility analysis. The design requirements control the design of the project throughout the engineering design process. Some design requirements include hardware and software parameters, maintainability, availability, and testability.

5. Preliminary design

The preliminary design bridges the gap between the design concept and the detailed design phase. In this task, the overall system configuration is defined, and schematics, diagrams, and layouts of the project will provide early project configuration. During detailed design and optimization, the parameters of the part being created will change, but the preliminary design focuses on creating the general framework to build the project on.

6. Detailed design

The detailed design portion of the engineering design process is the task where the engineer can completely describe a product through solid modeling and drawings. Some specifications include
- Operating parameters.
- Operating and nonoperating environmental stimuli.
- Test requirements.
- External dimensions.
- Maintenance and testability provisions.
- Materials requirements.
- Reliability requirements.
- External surface treatment.

- Design life.
- Packaging requirements.
- External marking.

The advancement of computer-aided design, or CAD, programs have made the detailed design phase more efficient. This is because a CAD program can provide optimization, where it can reduce volume without hindering the part's quality. It can also calculate stress and displacement using the finite element method to determine stresses throughout the part. It is the engineer's responsibility to determine whether these stresses and displacements are allowable, so the part is safe.

7. Production planning and tool design

The production planning and tool design is nothing more than planning how to <u>mass-produce</u> the project and which tools should be used in the manufacturing of the part. Tasks to complete in this step include selecting the material, selection of the production processes, determination of the sequence of operations, and selection of tools, such as jigs, fixtures, and tooling. This task also involves testing a working prototype to ensure the created part meeting qualification standards.

8. Production

With the completion of qualification testing and prototype testing, the engineering design process is <u>finalized</u>. The part must now be manufactured, and the machines must be inspected regularly to make sure that they do not break down and slow production.

(989 words)

A. *Summarize each part of the engineering design process.*

B. *Collocations*:

creativity	open-ended
design theory and methodology	optimization
optimally	solutions
statements and specification	qualification standards

1) Be applied to convert resources _____ to meet a stated objective.
2) Development of student _____.
3) Use of _____ problems.
4) Development and use of modern _____.
5) Formulation of design problem _____.
6) Consideration of alternative _____.
7) To ensure the created part meets _____.
8) A CAD program can provide _____.

C. *Use words you have learnt to explain the underlined words in the sentences below.*

1) The engineering design process is a <u>multi-step</u> process including the research,

conceptualization, feasibility assessment, establishing design requirements, preliminary design, detailed design, production planning and tool design, and finally production.

2) Consideration should be given to the existing <u>applicable</u> literature, problems and successes associated with existing solutions, costs, and marketplace needs.

3) The vital aspect of the <u>conceptualization</u> step is synthesis.

4) The purpose of a <u>feasibility</u> assessment is to determine whether the engineer's project can proceed into the design phase.

5) This is based on two criterias: the project needs to be based on an achievable idea, and it needs to be within cost <u>constraints</u>.

6) The preliminary design <u>bridges the gap</u> between the design concept and the detailed design phase.

7) The production planning and tool design is nothing more than planning how to <u>mass-produce</u> the project and which tools should be used in the manufacturing of the part.

8) With the completion of qualification testing and prototype testing, the engineering design process is <u>finalized</u>.

Culture Notes

TenStep Project Definition

The TenStep Project Management Process (TenStep) is designed to provide the information you need to be a successful Project Manager, including a step-by-step approach, starting with the basics and getting as sophisticated as you need for your particular project. TenStep is a flexible and scalable methodology for managing work as a project. The basic philosophy is "large methodology for large projects, small methodology for small projects". TenStep shows you what you need to know to manage projects of all size.

Part Two Writing

Writing Skills: Emails

- **Subjects**

Give the message a subject/title. Email messages without a subject may not be opened because of a fear of viruses and especially note that it is very easy to forget to type in this important information.

- **Subject contents**

Keep the subject short and clear but avoid such headings as: Good News, Hello, and Message from Mary. These headings are common in messages containing viruses. Short but specific headings are needed, e.g. Order No. 213D, Delayed Shipment, Office meeting postponed.

- **Greetings**

Start the message with a greeting so as to help create a friendly but business-like tone. The choice of using the other name versus the surname will depend on who you are writing to. If you have communicated with the receiver previously and he/she is at a similar level to you, then the use of the other name would be appropriate. If the receiver is more senior to you, or if you are in doubt, it would be safer (particularly in the first communication) to use the person's surname/family name together with a title, e.g. Dear Mr Smithson, Dear Ms Stringer.

It is also becoming quite common to write the greeting without a comma, e.g. Dear Miss Lawson.

- **Purpose**

Start with a clear indication of what the message is about in the first paragraph.

Give full details in the following paragraph(s).

Make sure that the final paragraph indicates what should happen next, e.g. "I will send a messenger to your office on Tuesday morning to collect the faulty goods" or "Please let me have your order by the beginning of the month".

- **Action**

Any action that you want the reader to do should be clearly described, using politeness phrases. Subordinates should use expressions such as "Could you..." or "I would be grateful if...". Superior staff should also use polite phrases, for example, "Please...".

- **Attachments**

Make sure you refer, in the main message, to any attachments you are adding and of course make extra sure that you remember to include the attachment(s). As attachments can transmit viruses, try not to use them, unless you are sending complicated documents. Copy-and-paste text-only contents into the body of the email. If you use an attachment, make sure the file name describes the content, and is not too general; e.g. "message.doc" is bad, but "QA Report 2014.doc" is good.

- **Endings**

End the message in a polite way. Common endings are: Yours sincerely, Best regards, Best wishes, Regards.

If you did not put a comma after the greeting at the beginning of the message, then do not put a comma after the ending either, e.g. "Best wishes" or "Regards".

- **Names**

Include your name at the end of the message. It is most annoying to receive an email which does not include the name of the sender. The problem is that often the email address of the sender does not indicate exactly who it is from.

I. Sample 1

To: aadams@adamsofficesolutions.com
From: jjames@adamsofficesolutions.com

Subject: Meeting About New Internet Service Provider 12 April, 2014

Mr. Adams,
I have been researching our choices for internet providers over the past week, and I wanted to update you on my progress. We have two options: H. C. Cable and Toll South. Both offer business plans, and I will go over the pricing of each plan at the meeting on Tuesday. Both of the options I listed have comparable speed and data usage offerings as well. I called your personal provider, GoGo Satellite, but they did not have any business offerings. They primarily do residential internet service.
I will talk with Joe and Susan in IT about these options and get their suggestions. I will also send out meeting requests to everyone, including Mr. Morris in operations. If you have any questions prior to the meeting, please let me know.

Respectfully,

Jolin James
Administrative Assistant
Adams Office Solutions
http://www.adamsofficesolutions.com
(555) 124-5678

II. Sample 2

Dear Ms. Smith,

Thank you for your email; I am very grateful for your offer of an internship this summer. It was a pleasure meeting you and your colleagues and learning more about the work of your office.
After careful consideration, I write to let you know that I must decline your offer. While I am inspired by the work that you do on the national level and hope to contribute to your mission in the future, I have decided to pursue an opportunity that affords me the chance to work one-on-one with clients.

> Thank you so much for your time and consideration.
>
> Sincerely,
> John Harvard

III. Exercise

You are writing to Ms. Smith to request more time to consider an offer, either for personal reasons or because you are juggling other offers and interviews. You may politely ask for more time.

Part Three　Case Study

For web designers, having successful client projects direct to happy clients, more recommendations, an established track record, and priceless experience and knowledge that can be used in upcoming projects. But there is a lot that goes into building a project a success, and just finishing the design on time is not sufficient. You have to design your projects in the most featured way to make your projects more flourishing. In order to create a website that exploits its prospective for your client, you'll first have to get a clear admiring of the client, i. e. how they do business, how they sort themselves, and you'll also need to become well-known with their target market. Depending on your familiarity with the client and their industry, this may necessitate a substantial amount of time and effort. The better understanding you have, the more probably you will be able to create sites that convene the needs of the client and their end users.

Many clients begin the website development process with a definite style in mind. They have likely seen a little websites online that have a common look that they will like to track. Otherwise, if you have developed a special style, you can win over more of the clients that are hopeful to create comparable sites. You won't get clients seeming for other styles, but you also won't have to match a range of different styles. By choosing between these two advances, you should embrace the site designs in your project, which finally comes down to a question of, the type of sites you desire to work in the future. While designing the project for your clients you should be principally superior in case of specific skills. Contribution to a short description along with each website you include in your project is the easiest approach, particularly if you are already preparing on including information like the date and tools used.

A. *Answer the following questions:*

1) What are the elements that go into making a project success?
2) What is important thing to consider when you design a website for your clients?

B. *You are describing your web design to your clients. Your description includes the answers to the following three questions.*

1) The ways you have used your abilities to speed up construction;
2) The ways your skills make a website set out;
3) The technologies you are mainly capable of.

Unit Seven

Coding

Note on the topic

软件编码是指将上一阶段的详细设计得到的处理过程的描述转换为基于某种计算机语言的程序,即源程序代码。软件工程师根据项目的应用领域选择适当的编程语言。编程的软硬件环境以及编码的程序设计风格等事项在编程过程中也很重要。软件编码是系统设计过程的继续,是将软件设计转化成用程序设计语言编写的源程序的过程,加以更正、改良。

只要是一个有用的软件就需要大量的工作,首先要进行软件需求分析,然后要设计出软件的框架,而实现软件的代码仅占很少一部分。但你不要小看这代码的实现,要很多人的参与,一般软件代码就有上千行,更别说操作系统了。计算机是如何读懂并执行输入给它的命令的呢?编码技术的好坏有多重要?读读本章的内容,你就能回答这些问题。

Part One Reading

I. Before you read

A. *Discuss the following questions in a group.*

1) What is coding?

2) Is there any difference between coding and programming?

3) What are the common programming languages you know? Below are listed the commonly used programming languages. Which one/ones are you familiar with? Which one/ones have you used? Which one/ones you have never heard of?

C	Python	Java	PHP	Perl	C++
JavaScript	C-Sharp	Ruby	Objective-C	Visual Basic	SQL

4) Below are the descriptions of the programming languages. The letter "X" is used to refer to one of the languages. Find out what "X" is for each description and choose your answer from the box above in exercise 3. Search online if necessary.

X1 is a very prominent programming language for websites that first appeared in 1995. X is a high-level interpreted scripting language. Its main platform is web browsers, but it's also gained recent popularity on web servers through Node. js.
X2 is a high-level interpreted programming language that runs on a range of different platforms. It was created in 1991 by Guido van Rossum. It was designed to emphasize code readability, with clear and expressive syntax. A lot of people choose to learn it first for this very reason.
X3 stands for Structured Query Language. It's been used to interact with databases since 1974. It is often written as standalone lines known as queries. Each query is designed to either create, read, update or delete data in a database.
X4 is a programming language for producing dynamic web pages. It was created by Rasmus Lerdorf in 1995. It has the abilities to send SQL queries and to output HTML, and can be described as the link between the database that stores all the content on a site, and the HTML that lets you view it. Its platform is the web server. It's a high-level interpreted scripting language, but it has the lowest-level access of any web server language.
X5 was created in 1995 by Yukihiro Matsumoto. It was designed to be fun and productive to program in, with the needs of programmers—rather than computers—in mind. It is a high-level interpreted language that's gained popularity on the web through the Ruby on Rails framework.
Arguably, the daddy of modern programming languages is X6. It has been around since 1972, and although it's not easy to learn, it's extremely powerful. It is a compiled language and the lowest-level of all the languages listed here. It's readily built into nearly every operating system.
X7 is an enhanced version of C that adds the object-oriented paradigm. It was created by Bjarne Stroustrup in 1979. It is a compiled language and runs on multiple hardware platforms.
X8, like C++, has its roots in C. Also written C#, the language was developed by Microsoft in 2000 and is used extensively in its .NET framework. It is a compiled high-level language and runs on Windows only.
X9 is another Microsoft language, developed in 1991. It is an event-driven language, meaning it's designed to respond to user events such as mouse clicks or key presses. It is a high-level compiled language and its platform is Windows.
X10 is a ubiquitous programming language designed for cross-platform compatibility. It was developed by Oracle Corporation and first appeared in 1995. It is a high-level compiled language and is designed to run on just about any operating system.
X11, like C++ and C#, was derived from the C language. It was developed by Apple in 1983 and is designed to be used in conjunction with the company's Cocoa framework. It is a high-level compiled language and runs only on Apple operating systems.
X12 is a web language that was developed by Larry Wall in 1987. It's a powerful and practical language that was originally designed for text processing. It has been called "the duct tape that holds the Internet together", referring to its power and perceived ugliness. It is a high-level interpreted language and has been used extensively on the web.

B. *KEYS*

X1 JavaScript	X4 PHP	X7 C++	X10 Java
X2 Python	X5 Ruby	X8 C-Sharp	X11 Objective-C
X3 SQL	X6 C	X9 Visual Basic	X12 Perl

II. Text Reading

How Programming Works

How does coding work, really?

The short answer is that writing code tells the computer what to do, but it's not quite that simple. So here's the longer answer. A computer can only understand two distinct types of data: on and off.

In fact, a computer is really just a collection of on/off switches (**transistors**). Anything that a computer can do is nothing more than a unique combination of some transistors turned on and some transistors turned off.

Binary code is the representation of these combinations as 1s and 0s, where each **digit** represents one transistor. Binary code is grouped into bytes, groups of 8 digits representing 8 transistors, for example, 11101001. Modern computers contain millions or even billions of transistors, which means an unimaginably large number of combinations.

But one problem **arises** here. To be able to write a computer program by typing out billions of 1s and 0s would require superhuman brainpower, and even then it would probably take you a lifetime or two to write. This is where programming languages come in...

Here's a simple example of some code: print "Hello, world!"

That line of code is written in the Python programming language. Put simply, a programming language is a set of **syntax** rules that define how code should be written and formatted.

Programming languages are what make it possible for us to create computer software, apps and websites. Instead of writing binary code, they let us write code that is (relatively) easy for us to write, read and understand.

Each of the thousands of programming languages comes with a special program that takes care of translating what we write into binary code.

Why do we have so many programming languages? Because different languages are designed to be used for different purposes—some are useful for web development, others are useful for writing desktop software, others are useful for solving scientific and **numeric** problems, and so on.

Programming languages can also be low-level or high-level. Low-level languages are closer to the binary code a computer understands, while high-level languages bear a lot less **resemblance** to binary code.

High-level languages are easier to program in, because they're less detailed and designed to be easy for us to write. Nearly all of the main programming languages in use today are high-level languages.

A program is simply a text file, written in a certain programming language. The code inside a program file is called the source code. Every programming language has its own file extension for identifying code files written in that language. For example, Python's is ". py".

To make a program, you write the code in a **plain** text editor like Notepad and save the file to your computer. That's it. For example, the below line of code could be the contents of a very short Python program called hello. py: print "Hello, world!"

How do you run a program and actually get it to perform its commands? That varies between programming languages.

Some languages save a separate binary file that the computer can directly run, while other languages have their programs run indirectly by certain software.

For example, a JavaScript program file would get run by a web browser like Chrome. A PHP program file would get run by a web server like LAMP.

In the case of our hello. py file, the Python language comes with a command line which will display the output of the program—the text "Hello, world!" If you were to enter the code into the command line and press enter, the program gets running and the command will get executed.

What happens when you run a program? A computer doesn't actually understand the phrase "Hello, world!", and it doesn't know how to display it on the screen. It only understands on and off. So to actually run a command like print "Hello, world", it has to translate all the code in a program into a series of ons and offs that it can understand.

To do that, a number of things happen:
1) The source code is translated into **assembly** language.
2) The assembly code is translated into machine language.
3) The machine language is directly **executed** as binary code.

Confused? Let's go into a bit more detail. The programming language first has to translate its source code into assembly language, a super low-level language that uses words and numbers to represent binary patterns. Depending on the programming language, this may be done with an interpreter (where the program is translated line-by-line), or with a **compiler** (where the program is translated as a whole).

The programming language then sends off the assembly code to the computer's assembler, which **converts** it into the machine language that the computer can understand and execute directly as binary code.

Isn't it amazing to think that something as **deceptively** simple and **primitive** as binary code can create things as complex as what goes on inside a computer?

Your screen, operating system, photos, videos, the Internet, Facebook, your online bank account, and this website—all these things can be constructed from nothing but 1s and 0s. It's a real symbol of human achievement.

Don't worry if this process seems complicated and confusing—the whole reason programming languages exist is to simplify it all for you!

(872 Words)

III. Words to Note

transistor	n.	晶体管
binary	a.	二进制的
digit	n.	数字
arise	v.	出现
syntax	n.	句法
numeric	a.	数字的,数值的
resemblance	n.	相似,相似物
plain	a.	简单的,朴素的
assembly	n.	装配
execute	v.	执行
compiler	n.	编译程序
convert	v.	转化
deceptively	adv.	欺骗性的
primitive	a.	原始的

IV. Text Understanding

Read the text and answer the following questions.

1) Why programming languages are necessary?

2) What is the difference between programming and coding?

3) What are the different purposes of different programming languages?

4) What are the advantages of using high-level languages?

5) How does a computer understand a "language"?

V. Vocabulary Building

A. *Use words and expressions from the text to replace the underlined words and expressions.*

1) Anything that a computer can do is nothing more than *the only one of its kind* combination of some transistors turned on and some transistors turned off.

2) Modern computers contain millions or even billions of transistors, which means an unimaginably large number of *mixtures*.

3) Low-level languages are closer to the binary code a computer understands, while high-level languages bear a lot less *similarities* to binary code.

4) Every programming language has its own file extension for identifying code files written in that language.

5) To make a program, you write the code in a *simple* text editor like Notepad and save the file to your computer.

6) If you were to enter the code into the command line and press enter, the program gets run and the command will get *carried out*.

7) The programming language then sends off the assembly code to the computer's assembler, which *changes* it into the machine language that the computer can understand and execute directly as binary code.

8) Isn't it amazing to think that something as *seemingly* simple and **primitive** as binary code can create things as complex as what goes on inside a computer?

B. Complete sentence with the words given.

| arise | resemblance | plain | convert |
| execute | assembly | deceptively | primitive |

1) Solar cells _____ sunlight to electricity.

2) We are going to _____ our campaign plan to the letter.

3) The new president may bear a striking _____ to the departing one.

4) An _____ language or two would do equally well.

5) Human emotions _____ from a network of interconnected brain regions.

6) Instead, some features shift to the advanced form at the beginning of the process, while others stay resolutely _____ until near the end.

7) Consider where the icebergs might be that you can't see, or where the threats might look _____ small on the surface.

8) From my office window, I can see a _____ mews building.

C. Translate the following paragraph into Chinese.

The programming language first has to translate its source code into assembly language, a super low-level language that uses words and numbers to represent binary patterns. Depending on the programming language, this may be done with an interpreter (where the program is translated line-by-line), or with a compiler (where the program is translated as a whole).

VI. Further Reading

Coding Techniques and Programming Practices

1. _____

Superior coding techniques and programming practices are hallmarks of a professional programmer. The bulk of programming consists of making a large number of small choices while attempting to solve a larger set of problems. How wisely those choices are made depends largely upon the programmer's skill and expertise.

This document addresses some fundamental coding techniques and provides a collection of coding practices from which to learn. The coding techniques are primarily those that improve the readability and maintainability of code, whereas the programming practices are mostly performance enhancements.

The readability of source code has a direct impact on how well a developer comprehends a software system. Code maintainability refers to how easily that software system can be changed to add new features, modify existing features, fix bugs, or improve performance. Although readability and maintainability are the results of many factors, one particular facet of software development upon which all developers have an influence is coding technique. The easiest method to ensure that a team of developers will yield quality code is to establish a coding standard, which is then enforced at routine code reviews.

2. _____

A comprehensive coding standard encompasses all aspects of code construction and, while developers should exercise prudence in its implementation, it should be closely followed.

Completed source code should reflect a harmonized style, as if a single developer wrote the code in one session. At the inception of a software project, establish a coding standard to ensure that all developers on the project are working in concert. When the software project will incorporate existing source code, or when performing maintenance upon an existing software system, the coding standard should state how to deal with the existing code base.

Although the primary purpose for conducting code reviews throughout the development life cycle is to identify defects in the code, the reviews can also be used to enforce coding standards in a uniform manner. Adherence to a coding standard can only be feasible when followed throughout the software project from inception to completion. It is not practical, nor is it prudent, to impose a coding standard after the fact.

3. _____

Coding techniques incorporate many facets of software development and, although they usually have no impact on the functionality of the application, they contribute to an improved comprehension of source code. For the purpose of this document, all forms of source code are considered, including programming, scripting, markup, and query languages.

The coding techniques defined here are not proposed to form an inflexible set of coding standards. Rather, they are meant to serve as a guide for developing a coding standard for a specific software project.

The coding techniques are divided into three sections: names, comments, format.

4. _____

Experienced developers follow numerous programming practices or <u>rules of thumb</u>, which typically derived from hard-learned lessons. The practices listed below are not all-inclusive, and should not be used without due consideration. Veteran programmers deviate from these practices on occasion, but not without careful consideration of the potential repercussions. Using the best programming practice in the wrong context can cause more harm than good.

5. _____

Using solid coding techniques and good programming practices to create high quality code plays an important role in software quality and performance. In addition, by consistently applying a well-defined coding standard and proper coding techniques, and holding routine code reviews, a team of programmers working on a software project is more likely to yield a software system that is easier to comprehend and maintain.

(510 words)

A. Skim the text. Match the main ideas a ~ e with corresponding parts 1 ~ 5.
a. Coding Standards and Code Reviews
b. Programming Practices
c. Conclusion
d. Introduction
e. Coding Techniques

B. Collocations:

superior	veteran
fundamental	potential
routine	solid
hard-learned	well-defined
proper	high quality

_____ coding techniques
_____ coding standard
_____ code review
_____ lessons
_____ programmers
_____ code
_____ repercussions

C. Use words you have learnt to explain the underlined words in the sentences below.

1) Superior coding techniques and programming practices are <u>hallmarks</u> of a professional programmer.

2) How wisely those choices are made depends largely upon the programmer's skill and <u>expertise</u>.

3) This document <u>addresses</u> some fundamental coding techniques and provides a collection of coding practices from which to learn.

4) The readability of source code has a direct impact on how well a developer <u>comprehends</u> a software system.

5) A comprehensive coding standard encompasses all aspects of code construction and, while developers should exercise <u>prudence</u> in its implementation, it should be closely followed.

6) At the inception of a software project, establish a coding standard to ensure that all developers on the project are <u>working in concert</u>.

7) Coding techniques incorporate many <u>facets</u> of software development and, although they usually have no impact on the functionality of the application, they contribute to an improved comprehension of source code.

8) Experienced developers follow numerous programming practices or <u>rules of thumb</u>, which typically derived from <u>hard-learned</u> lessons.

Cultural Notes

Hacker subculture

As a subculture, hackers have developed a particular sense of style that has been transformed over time and has been structured as an increasingly fluid and powerful form of resistance. As a youth culture, hackers are continually looking for ways to perturb or disrupt authority and challenge any understanding or representation of who they are. Hackers are not the only youth culture online. In fact, youth culture seems to have found the Internet to be the preferred medium for expression.

Issues that have typically represented youth culture-rebellion, resistance, fan culture, music, fashion, and pop culture; all find expression in Social networks, Internet chat rooms, World Wide Web pages, email mailing lists, forums and assorted other online elements. Hackers, however, illustrate a particular aspect of online culture that is more properly called a subculture, a culture that is both inherently tied to a larger, in this case, parental culture, but also resistant to it. The importance of online culture—particularly in the 1980s, 1990s, and up to the present—for youth culture is grounded in three factors. First, for the youth technology represents a way of doing things, a style, that is radically different from that of their parents. Second, Computer culture and computer style are in many ways the ideal hotbed for youth rebellion, as they require constant change in keeping with hardware and software developments. Third, the semiotic space that technology presents is one that is considerably less material than the traditional outlets of expression. Fashion, music, and literature, three primary outlets of youth culture expression, require a primary material component that is able to be marked, transformed, or reappropriated by mainstream culture. Computer culture, in contrast, is much less material in nature.

Part Two Writing

Writing skills: Meeting Minutes

I. What are meeting minutes

Minutes of a meeting, as we all know, are a record of all that was discussed, argued and concluded in a meeting. These minutes are recorded usually by the secretary, and are later summarized and recorded more professionally for approval. Once the recording is complete, these minutes are later sent to all those who attended the meeting, as well as other concerned people, if any. Meeting minutes are very important to an organization. A company spends a lot of time during a meeting, and every single minute is spent on discussing something important; a decision that might influence a lot of people. It is human nature to forget small details that might be important otherwise. For this very reason, the meetings of a minute have such high value. In the paragraphs below, we'll first learn how you can design your own template. Second, we'll see a template that implements the points you note. Third, we'll understand this same template further, through a sample.

II. How to Design your Own Minutes of Meeting Format

First, write down all the basic details you will need for designing the format. These will include things like name of the body holding the meeting, the date, time, location, etc.

Now, make a list of people who are expected to be present at the meeting. Ask the person in charge of the meeting for this list or, you can also refer to the minutes of the previous meeting, if this one is in continuation.

Agenda of the meeting is the most important aspect of the minutes. Writing down the correct points of discussion is very crucial. Cross-check time and again to be sure that you haven't missed anything.

When a point is discussed, write down only the key points of that discussion. This will help you summarize better. Write down the conclusion attendees arrive at. With the conclusion, you will also have to write the detailed vote. This means who voted in favor of the decision and who voted against it.

You must remember that these minutes, once properly drafted, need official approval. For them to be approved, you need to provide all correct details. Remember, only approved minutes can be used as reference material in the future.

Ⅲ. Sample Writing

Quarterly Creative Department Analysis Meeting Minutes		
Date: March 20, 2014	Time: 08:30 am.	Location: Conference Room 3A
Meeting Called By: Mr. James Clark, Director, Communications Type of Meeting: Quarterly Facilitator: Mr. Sam Mathew, Creative Director Note Taker: Miss Rachel Joseph, Secretary to Managing Director		
Attendees		
☑Name 1:		☑Name 2:
☑Name 3:		☑Name 4:
☑Name 5:		☑Name 6:
☒Name 7:		☒Name 8:
☑Name 9:		☑Name 10:
*Click check box if the person is present.		
AGENDA		
1. To divide the department into specific teams with more specific tasks.		
2. To arrange for a workshop that motivates employees and enhances their creativity once every month.		
3. Hiring new people to increase output, thus not compromising on current quality standards.		
4. To increase concentration on global trends.		
5. To start a new department that will handle the company's profile on social media channels.		
DISCUSSIONS		
Topic: Starting a Social Media Department		
Comments: JC: Social Media has become an important part in the success of a company today and building it adds to the image of a company. SS: However, spending on it would be impossible before the next quarter ends. Also, the decision of starting or not must be taken now so as to start hiring. JC: A company's success isn't the gift of Social Media though it can definitely help create awareness about the company and thus add to its identity and help us in the future.		
Conclusion: Social Media department starts on 1st week of Q3 and hiring starts in 5th week on Q2.		

Vote	JC	☑	SM	☒
	SS	☑	PR	☐

ACTIONS
Topic 1: Design an advertisement for hiring Social Media Managers

续表

In charge: Katie Adams	Deadline: May 10, 2013
Topic 2: Creating a POA for the Social Media Team	
In charge: John Diaz	Deadline: May 10, 2013

IV. Exercise

A. *Answer the questions based on the sample above.*

1) When was the meeting?
2) Who attended?
3) Who did not attend? (Include this information if it matters.)
4) What topics were discussed?
5) What was decided?
6) What actions were agreed upon?
7) Who is to complete the actions, by when?

B. *Following statements are the Do's and Don'ts when writing meeting minutes. Tick "√" the answer/answers for "do's", and cross "×" the one/ones for "don'ts"*

☐ Write minutes soon after the meeting—preferably within 48 hours. That way, those who attended can be reminded of action items, and those who did not attend will promptly know what happened.

☐ Skip writing minutes just because everyone attended the meeting and knows what happened. Meeting notes serve as a record of the meeting long after people forget what happened.

☐ Describe all the "he said, she said" details unless those details are very important. Record topics discussed, decisions made, and action items.

☐ Include any information that will embarrass anyone (for example, "Then Terry left the room in tears").

☐ Use positive language. Rather than describing the discussion as *heated or angry*, use *passionate*, *lively*, or *energetic*—all of which are just as true as the negative words.

☐ Have a new year filled with productive meetings captured efficiently in crisp, clear meeting notes!

Part Three Case Study

I. Coding Guidelines for Cocoa

Developing a Cocoa framework, plug-in, or other executable with a public API requires some approaches and conventions that are different from those used in application development. The primary clients of your product are developers, and it is important that they are not mystified by your programmatic interface. This is where API naming conventions come in handy, for they help you to make your interfaces consistent and clear. There are also programming techniques that are special to—or of greater importance with—frameworks, such as versioning, binary compatibility, error-handling, andmemory management. This topic includes information on both Cocoa naming conventions and recommended programming practices for frameworks.

II. General Principles

Principle 1 _____

Code	Commentary
insertObject: atIndex	Good
insert: at	Not clear; what is being inserted? What does "at" signify
removeObjectAtIndex	Good
removeObject	Good, because it removes object referred to in argument
remove	Not clear; what is being removed

In general, don't abbreviate names of things. Spell them out, even if they're long:

Code	Commentary
destinationSelection	Good
destSel	Not clear
setBackgroundColor	Good
setBkgdColor	Not clear

You may think an abbreviation is well-known, but it might not be, especially if the developer encountering your method or function name has a different cultural and linguistic background.

However, a handful of abbreviations are truly common and have a long history of use. You can continue to use them. Avoid ambiguity in API names, such as method names that could be interpreted in more than one way.

Code	Commentary
sendPort	Does it send the port or return it
displayName	Does it display a name or return the receiver's title in the user interface

Principle 2 _____

Try to use names consistently throughout the Cocoa programmatic interfaces. If you are unsure, browse the current header files or reference documentation for precedents.

Consistency is especially important when you have a class whose methods should take advantage of polymorphism. Methods that do the same thing in different classes should have the same name.

Code	Commentary
- (NSInteger) tag	Defined in NSView, NSCell, NSControl
- (void) setStringValue:(NSString *)	Defined in a number of Cocoa classes

Principle 3 _____

Code	Commentary
NSString	Okay
NSStringObject	Self-referential

III. Team Activity

Read the codes and commentary below. Discuss in a group: What are the principles of Cocoa? Summarize the principles and fill in the blanks.

IV. Assignment

Introduce another coding style which might be different from Cocoa. Use specific examples to illustrate your idea.

Unit Eight

Software Testing

Note on the topic

软件开发的过程是分阶段实施的,而软件质量控制则贯穿于软件产品开发的整个生命周期。软件测试是为了发现错误而执行程序的过程。目的是为了在软件投入生产性运行之前,尽可能多地发现并排除软件中潜藏的错误,从而提高软件质量。软件生存期的各个阶段都可能产生错误,而软件需求分析、设计和实现阶段是软件的主要出错来源。

通过分析错误产生的原因,可以帮助发现当前开发工作所采用的软件过程的缺陷,以便进行软件过程改进。同时,通过对测试结果的分析整理,还可以修正软件开发规则,并为软件可靠性分析提供依据。它是帮助识别开发完成(中间或最终的版本)的计算机软件(整体或部分)的正确度(correctness)、完全度(completeness) 和质量(quality)的软件过程;是 SQA(Software Quality Assurance)的重要子域。

Part One   Reading

Ⅰ. Before you read

A. *Read the following events. What conclusion we can draw from the stories ?*

1994 年,美国迪斯尼公司发布了面向少年儿童的多媒体游戏软件——"狮子王动画故事书"。软件销售情况异常火爆,几乎成了当年秋季全美少年儿童必买的游戏。但产品开始销售后不久,该公司客户支持部门的电话就开始响个不停,玩不成游戏的孩子们及其家长大量投诉该游戏软件的缺陷。经调查证实,迪斯尼公司没有在该游戏软件可能使用的、市场已有的各种 PC上进行全面的测试,也就是说,游戏软件对硬件环境的兼容性没有得到保证。这个软件故障使迪斯尼公司的声誉受到很大损伤,迪斯尼公司为改正该软件的缺陷和故障也付出了极大的人力财力代价。

美国爱国者导弹系统开发完成后的首次应用是在海湾战争中,其功能就是对抗伊拉克的飞毛腿导弹系统。尽管爱国者导弹系统在这次战争中屡建奇功,多次成功拦截飞毛腿导弹,但也有几次在对抗的时候失利,其中竟然出现一枚爱国者导弹在沙特阿拉伯的多哈美国军营内爆炸,给美国人自己造成了严重伤害,付出了惨重代价。事后,专家对事故原因经过仔细的研究分析,得出的结论是:爱国者导弹防御系统中一个软件的缺陷造成了这次重大事故。这是一个很小的系统时钟错误,但积累下来可能延时 14 小时,从而造成跟踪系统失去准确度。在多哈事故中,导弹系统的重要时刻竟被延时了 100 多个小时,所以导致事故发生。

B. Discuss in a group: How important is software testing?

1) How many types of software testing do you know? Introduce them briefly.
2) What do you think are the most important elements for software testing?
3) Match the definition with the following terms.
   - A test strategy _____.
   - A testing plan _____.
   - Test cases _____.
   - Test data _____.
   - A test environment _____.

---

a. that have been prepared in advance in the form of detailed examples you will use to check that the software will actually meet its requirements

b. the actual testing tasks you will need to execute to carry out that strategy

c. that is consisted of both input test data and database test data to use while you are executing your test cases

d. where you will use to carry out your testing

e. that tells you what types of testing and the amount of testing you think will work best at finding the defects that are lurking in the software

---

Ⅱ. Text Reading

The Five Essentials for Software Testing

Five essential elements are required for successful software testing: test strategy, testing plan, test cases, test data and test environment. If any one of these five elements is missing or inadequate, your test effort will most likely fall far short of what you could otherwise achieve.

The following advice should help clarify your thinking about software testing and help you improve the effectiveness and efficiency of your testing. It is helpful to think about software testing in terms of five essential elements. If any one of these five elements is missing or inadequate, your test effort will most likely fall far short of what you could otherwise achieve.

A. *Test Strategy*

The purpose of testing is to find **defects**, not to pass easy tests. A test strategy basically tells you what types of testing seem best to do, the order in which to perform them, the proposed **sequence** of **execution**, and the **optimum** amount of effort to put into each test objective to make your testing most effective. A test strategy is based on the prioritized requirements and any other available information about what is important to the customers. Because you will always face time and resource constraints, a test strategy faces up to this reality and tells you how to make the best use of whatever resources you do have to locate most of the worst defects. Without a test strategy, you are apt to waste your time on less fruitful testing and miss using some of your most powerful testing options. You should create the test strategy at about the middle of the design phase as soon as the requirements have settled down.

B. *Testing Plan*

A testing plan is simply that part of your project plan that deals with the testing tasks. It details who will do which tasks, starting when, ending when, taking how much effort, and depending on which other tasks. It provides a complete list of all the things that need to be done for testing, including all the preparation work during all of the phases before testing. It shows the **dependencies** among the tasks to clearly create a critical path without surprises. You will be able to start filling in the details of your testing plan as soon as your test strategy is completed. Both your test strategy and testing plan are subject to change as the project evolves. **Modify** your strategy first, if you need to, and then your testing plan.

C. *Test Cases*

Your test cases (and **automated** test **scripts** if called for by your strategy) are prepared based on the strategy which tells you how much of each type of testing to do. Test cases are developed based on prioritized requirements and acceptance **criteria** for the software, keeping in mind the customer's emphasis on quality dimensions and the project's latest risk assessment of what could go wrong. Except for a small amount of **ad hoc** testing, all of your test cases should be prepared in advance of the start of testing. There are many different approaches to developing test cases. Test case development is an activity performed in **parallel** with software development. It is just as difficult to do a good job of coming up with test cases as it is to program the system itself. In addition to figuring out what steps to take to test the system, you need to know the requirements and business rules well enough to predict exactly what the expected results should be. Without expected results to compare to actual results, you will not be able to say whether a test will pass or fail. A good test case checks to make sure requirements are being met and has a good chance of uncovering defects.

D. *Test Data*

In addition to the steps to perform to execute your test cases, you also need to systematically come up with test data to use. This often equals sets of names, addresses, product orders, or whatever other information the system uses. Since you are probably going to test query functions, change functions and delete functions, you will most likely need a starting database of data in addition to the examples to input. Consider how many times you might need to go back to the starting point of the database to restart the testing and how many new customer names you will need for all the testing in your plan. Test data development is usually done **simultaneously** with test case development.

E. *Test Environment*

You will need a place to do the testing and the right equipment to use. Unless the software is very simple, one PC will not **suffice**. You will need all of the components of the system as close as possible to what it will eventually be. Test environments may be **scaled-down** versions of the real thing, but all the parts need to be there for the system to actually run. Building a test environment usually involves setting aside separate regions on **mainframe** computers and/or servers, networks and PCs that can be dedicated to the test effort and that can be reset to restart testing as often as needed. Sometimes lab rooms of equipment are set aside, especially for performance or usability testing. A wish list of components that will be needed is parts of the test strategy, which then needs to be reality checked as part of the test planning process. Steps to set up the environment are parts of the testing plan and need to be completed before testing begins.

F. *Conclusion*

If you want to improve your software testing, or if you are new to software testing, one very helpful thing you can do is to make sure you have all five of these essentials well in place. Many testers struggle with **inadequate** resources, undocumented requirements, and lack of involvement with the development process early in the software development life cycle. Pushing for all five of the essentials and proper timing are the only way to significantly improve the effectiveness of testing as an essential part of software engineering.

(1000 Words)

III. Words to Note

defect	n.	缺陷
sequence	n.	顺序
execution	n.	执行
optimum	a.	最适宜的
dependency	n.	相关信息
modify	v.	修改
automated	a.	自动化的
script	n.	脚本
criteria	n.	标准,条件

续表

ad hoc	a.	特别的,点对点的
parallel	n.	平行
simultaneously	a.	同时地
suffice	v.	满足
scaled-down	a.	按比例缩小
mainframe	n.	主机
inadequate	a.	不充分的,不适当的

IV. Text Understanding

Fill in the blanks based on the text.

1) A test strategy makes the testing process _____, and avoid _____.

2) A test plan enables you to _____. Both a test strategy and test plan need to be _____ as the project evolves.

3) Test case development is performed _____ software development. Test cases are developed based on customer's requirement on _____. A good test case ensures that _____.

4) Test data development is usually finished _____.

5) Building a test environment usually involves _____, _____, and _____.

V. Vocabulary Building

A. *Math the words with their definitions.*

parallel	a.	One thing happens at the same time or is similar with another, and the two often seem to be connected.
inadequate	b.	Be sufficient; be adequate, either in quality or quantity.
sequence	c.	At the same instant.
modify	d.	A basis for comparison; a reference point against which other things can be evaluated.
simultaneously	e.	The action of following in order.
suffice	f.	(Computer science) the process of carrying out an instruction by a computer.
criteria	g.	Not meeting the requirements especially of a task.
execution	h.	Change something slightly, usually in order to improve it.

B. *Complete sentence with the words given.*

parallel	sequence	simultaneously	suffice
criteria	execution	inadequate	modify

1) All of these capabilities make the test easier to follow during _____.

2) This technique fulfills most or all of the requirements of this evaluation _____.

3) If Spain falls into crisis, then all current mechanisms for dealing with the crisis will turn out to be _____.

4) We had to slightly _____ the original design.

5) Development of both the client and server side can then begin in _____.

6) Now, add this information to server in the following _____.

7) This allows several users to connect to the same desktop _____.

8) A cover letter should never exceed one page; often a far shorter letter will _____.

C. Translate the following paragraph into Chinese.

If you want to improve your software testing, or if you are new to software testing, one very helpful thing you can do is to make sure you have all five of these essentials well in place. Many testers struggle with **inadequate** resources, undocumented requirements, and lack of involvement with the development process early in the software development life cycle. Pushing for all five of the essentials and proper timing are the only way to significantly improve the effectiveness of testing as an essential part of software engineering.

VI. Further Reading

What Does a Software Test Engineer Do?

A software test engineer is usually responsible for testing new computer software or programs before the product is sold to consumers to ensure that it works properly, performs the desired functions, and is free from defects. These computer professionals usually design and perform the tests, evaluate the results, and make recommendations based on final conclusions. They often work as part of a quality assurance team, and work cooperatively with other quality assurance personnel such as computer programmers.

The software test engineer is involved in multiple phases of the development process, since new products must be tested continuously at various stages so that problems can be found and fixed quickly. New software is usually tested during several development phases including design, programming, installation, and maintenance. Software test engineers try to simulate many different usage scenarios to determine if the software performs as intended. They specifically check to see if the software accurately performs the functions it is designed for, and if it performs them in a reliable, consistent manner without any major difficulties. They also test for internet security issues.

There are two primary points of view a software test engineer uses while testing called white and black box testing. During white box testing, the tester uses an internal point of view. This means he or she is evaluating the structure of the programming, and is actually able to track the flow of information through the software and pinpoint where issues occur within the program.

In black box testing, the software test engineer assumes an external point of view, or the point of view of the software user. This means that he or she is testing as many different inputs of information as possible and evaluating the results of those inputs, but can't see exactly where things go wrong if problems do occur.

Once testing is completed, a software test engineer is responsible for evaluating and analyzing the results. Often, he or she will then work on designing solutions to any flaws that are found, as well as ways to improve the software's performance. The results and suggested solutions are communicated to other members of the quality assurance team, and the improvements are usually implemented by programmers. After that, the software is tested and evaluated again to determine if the improvements have the desired effect. The process continues until the team members are satisfied that the software is performing to expectations.

Software test engineers are usually employed by companies that produce and sell computer software or for consulting firms that are hired by the software companies. The work environment is usually an office, although in some cases working from home is possible. The work they perform is increasingly important and valuable as society grows more and more dependent on properly functioning computers in all walks of life.

(466 Words)

A. Decide whether the following statements are true or false based on the text. Tick "√" in the box if the statement is right; cross "×" if it is wrong.

☐ A software test engineer is responsible for testing new computer software or programs before the product is sold to consumers.

☐ Software testers design and perform the tests, evaluate the results, and make recommendations based on final conclusions.

☐ They often work cooperatively with other quality assurance personnel.

☐ The software test engineer is the last phase of the development process.

☐ They check to see if the software accurately performs the functions without any difficulties.

☐ They also test for internet security issues.

☐ During white box testing, the tester uses an external point of view; in black box testing, he or she assumes an external point of view.

☐ A tester will communicate to the quality assurance personnel when flaws are found, and ensure that they improve the software's performance.

B. Discuss the questions below in a group; write your main points briefly.

1) What makes a good software tester?

2) What are the advantages and disadvantages of a black box test and a white box test respectively?

C. *Read the following passage about things a software tester do every day. Choose a title that best summarizes the main idea for each part.*

a. Writing Test and Software Language
b. Removing Bugs and Defects in Software
c. Examine Software Using Black and White Box Testing
d. Write Documentation of Software Problems
e. Meet Clients, Employers and Software Designer

1. _____

A small portion of a software tester's day is filled with writing programming language. Testers who are using white-box testing methods may be asked to fill in missing code that creates an error message when simple tasks are completed. A software tester may be asked to write code for testing protocols and scripts based on her knowledge of a certain project. For example, a tester familiar with new hospital admittance software may be able to create protocols exposing bugs that disrupt file storage.

2. _____

Software testers spend most of their working days removing bugs and defects from programs. Every tester is given a list of numbers, words and commands that need to be entered into software. These data are designed to test programming language by creating thousands of different results, thereby testing the integration of individual components in software. A software tester may be asked to enter thousands of different words into a database program to determine the consequences of entering specific letter combinations.

3. _____

Software testers working on multiple projects at one time use black and white box testing regularly. Black box testing hides programming language from software testers, focusing the tester's attention on the execution of simple functions. White box testing exposes programming language and formats to the tester once black box testing has been completed successfully. After these testing methods are used, a software tester can run a final regression test to determine whether a program is ready for alpha (internal) and beta (public) testing. Regression testing runs through past sets of test data to determine whether software engineers caused additional problems by correcting programming language.

4. _____

Because software testers act as independent verifiers for unpublished programs, software companies ask for extensive documentation about testing processes. Every tester needs to keep track of individual test data used, errors found and time spent running these tests. This information is used by software engineers and designers after each test to clean up programming language before the next test. In the case of white box testing, an experienced tester can suggest specific lines of programming that need to be addressed to correct minor problems.

5. _____

Software testers stay in constant contact with developers, project managers and clients as they run through their processes. A tester must communicate ongoing problems with programming to developers in order to eliminate repeats of the same issues in future tests. Many testers use phone calls and online conferences to speak with managers and clients, outlining their test processes and offering insights into software performance. If a tester has full-time work with a software company, these meetings take place in teleconferencing centers and offices designed for virtual meetings.

Cultural Notes

> The separation of debugging from testing was initially introduced by Glenford J. Myers in 1979. Although his attention was on breakage testing ("a successful test is one that finds a bug") it illustrated the desire of the software engineering community to separate fundamental development activities, such as debugging, from that of verification. Dave Gelperin and William C. Hetzel classified in 1988 the phases and goals in software testing in the following stages:
>
> Until 1956—Debugging oriented.
> 1957—1978—Demonstration oriented.
> 1979—1982—Destruction oriented.
> 1983—1987—Evaluation oriented.
> 1988—2000—Prevention oriented.

Part Two   Writing

Writing Skills: How to Write Effective Emails to QA Team

What is the first thing you do when you get to work (or sometimes as soon as you wake up)? Check email, right? Sometimes we don't know what our day is going to be like until we read right through each email in the inbox, isn't it? In many of our earlier articles, we have highlighted the importance of good communication skill to effectively convey your message to your intended audience—one of the important soft skill for the testers.

In this part, we will focus on one specific section of written communication—i. e. email communication. We are sharing some tips and tricks to make email communication smoother and effective. This is applicable for all teams and not just the QA team.

Read the following two emails. What do you think of them? Which one do you think is more effective? Why?

I. Email 1

To: Testing Team
Subject: QA Update
Team,

There has been an unexpected delay in the deployment of code to the staging environment. For some reason the code got mixed up and we don't know when this issues will be sorted out. We are going to have to postpone our activities, don't know until when. So engage yourselves in other testing activities.
The change request CR0100H68 is in planned to hit production by the end of this month. Please go over the document from share point and give me an estimate.

Thanks,
X, QA team.

II. Email 2

To: Testing Team
Subject: Staging environment code deployment delayed—indefinitely & CR0100H68—need analysis

Hello Team,
Today, I've two updates for the team.
1) The staging environment deployment issues:
- Due to unexpected reasons the Staging environment code deployment is delayed—no ETA yet. We have to postpone our staging activities until we have further updates.
- Please work on creating the templates for the quality audit until it is resolved.
2) New update and tasks for changing request CR0100H68:
- Expected to go live by the end of the month.
- Please go over the documents and let me know the following details by EOD tomorrow.

- How many test scenarios do we need?
- How much of the existing documentation will we have to change?
- How much time it takes to write the new documentation?
- What are the test data requirements?
- How long is the test execution time?

Thanks,
X, QA team.

If you were a recipient of the email 1, what would happen? Finish the matching below, and you might be clearer about the problems existing in this email.

1) You might not even open it right away...
2) Even if you did open it...
3) You really have no idea what to do...

a. let's face it, it is just one big chunk of words; tedious, to say the least.
b. because the subject line does nothing to convey the importance of the content of the email.
c. the tasks to be done or the expectations from you are pretty vague.

But if you get email 2, you may find that:

1) You know what the email is about...
2) You grasp things easy...
3) You know what to do...

a. because the content is clearly organized in bulleted points.
b. because all the tasks to be done and the ETA are clearly defined.
c. because the subject line helps you correctly guess the tone of what's being communicated.

As you can see, taking simple measures has improved the quality of the communication. Here are some guidelines that can make email communication smoother and effective:

(1) Organize your thoughts before you start composing the email.
(2) Use the subject line to your benefit—Set the tone of what the email is going to contain. Give the recipients a sneak peak, if you will, into what's inside.
(3) Use the email program's "Important" flag to signal a critical communication—but again, be judicious in your decision as to what constitutes important. For example, if the testing cannot continue due to some error and all the teams need to know about it—

mark the email important.

(4) Define the intent of the email clearly.

- You are providing information—Be crisp about what you write. Keep it clear, keep it simple. Keep it concise.
- You are requesting information—What do you want, when do you want, how do you want it.

For example: I would like a copy of the Test plan document by the EOD. Please place the same in the common project folder and let me know.

- Acknowledgement—These are one liners and don't have much to them. Typically "Thank you" or "Done".

(5) Try to check spelling. Most email applications come with an option to perform this check mandatorily every time an email goes out.

(6) When you are in CC, it means it's a FYI. So you just need to know what's going on but an action from you is not expected.

(7) Do not reply all when not necessary.

(8) To avoid an email that you sent to multiple recipients be "replied to all", BCC all the email addresses.

(9) Be sensitive. When you are delivering a critical or negative feedback about a person or product, try to do it by talking to the person directly or send an email to just that person.

More tips to avoid the "Oops" moments:

(1) Put in the email address in the To, CC or BCC fields at last; once you have composed the email and are satisfied with the content you wrote. This is because, sometimes, you might accidentally hit "send" before you are ready and end up being the sender of an incomplete or incorrect email.

(2) When it does happen that you did send a half complete (or half incomplete, depending on your philosophical bent) email accidentally, there is a recall option available to make amends.

(3) If you are new at writing official emails—try to get a peer to read it for you before you send it and get his opinion.

(4) Do not use a colloquial expression or an idiom unless you know what it means. You might end up saying something embarrassing and an email once sent is pretty much set in stone.

Exercise

Write an email to a QA team based on the scenario below:

QA 发现系统在跑 service 的时候,客户存入账户的资金数额发生错误。经过调查,是数据库里的 frequency 字段的时间单位出现了问题——开发组（developers）在写代码的时候忽略了这一点，把程序写成了 hard code。作为 QA 组的成员，请写一封邮件给开发组，要求他们查询数据库，把正确的逻辑写进去。注意写清楚邮件的主题，并用数字标出几点要求和问题。

Part Three　Case Study

Years ago I worked on a new "next-generation" project at a software company. Everything seemed to be going well until the time came to do quality testing. As the software approached the test phase, the schedule looked pretty good. There had been some slips, but the project seemed on target for the scheduled release date. That is, until it actually went into testing.

On this project, testing had been treated as a black box. Software went into the lab, the testers did whatever it is that testers do, and bug reports came out. Since it was a black box, it was difficult for management to understand or justify time, resources, or equipment for testing. Also, nobody outside of the testing group, including project management, really understood what the process was or how to determine whether or not testing was complete. Several weeks were allocated to do a single test run, after which it was anticipated that the software would be ready to release.

Unfortunately, that was not the way the project went. Instead of a single pass through testing, ten different versions of the software required to complete testing runs. The schedule was hopelessly overrun, and instead of having a new release to announce at an important show, all the company had were some "closed-door" demos for selected customers.

Team Activity

　　Discuss in a group：

　　1) What the problems have arisen in the software release process?

　　2) What causes the problem?

　　3) How to solve the problem?

Unit Nine

Release Management

Note on the topic

在这一章里,我们将了解软件验收和交付过程中的主要流程和需要注意的问题,比如文档审核的重要性,更新软件发布的频率,以及在交付前要经历的几个阶段等。

读完这一章,我们就会对软件交付管理有基本的了解。

Part One　Reading

I. Before you read

Discuss the following questions in a group.
1) What is "release"?
2) How can we say a software is "ready" to be released?

II. Text Reading

Release Management

A system release is a version of the system that is distributed to customers. System release managers are responsible for deciding when the system can be released to customers, managing the process of creating the release and the distribution media, and documenting the release to ensure that it may be re-created exactly as distributed if this is necessary. A system release is not just the **executable** code of the system. The release may also include

- **Configuration** flies defining how the release should be configured for particular installations.
- Data files that are needed for successful system operation.
- An installation program that is used to help install the system on target hardware.
- Electronic and paper documentation describing the system.

- Packaging and associated **publicitxy** that have been designed for that release.

Release managers cannot assume that customers will always install new system releases. Some system users may be happy with an existing system. They may consider it not worth the cost of changing to a new release. New releases of the system cannot, therefore, rely on the installation of previous release. To illustrate this problem, consider the following **scenarioes**:

- Release 1 of a system is distributed and put into use.
- Release 2 requires the installation of new data files, but some customers do not need the facilities of release 2 to remain with release 1.
- Release 3 requires the data files installed in release 2 and has no new data files of its own.

The software distributor cannot assume that the files required for release 3 have already been installed in all sites. Some sites may go directly from release 1 to release 3, **skipping** release 2. Some sites may have modified the data files associated with release 2 to reflect local circumstances. Therefore, the data files must be distributed and installed with release 3 of the system.

Preparing and distributing a system release is an expensive process, particularly for mass-market software products. If releases are too frequent, customers may not **upgrade** to the new release, especially when it is not free. If system releases are **infrequent**, market share may be lost as customers move to **alternative** systems. This, of course, does not apply to custom software developed specially for an organization. For custom software, infrequent releases may mean increasing **divergence** between the software and the business processes that it is designed to support.

When a system release is produced, it must be documented to ensure that it can be re-created exactly in the future. This is particularly important for **customized**, long-lifetime **embedded** systems such as those controlling complex machines. Customers may use a single release of these systems for many years and may require specific changes to a particular software release long after its original release date.

To document a release, you have to record the specific versions of the source code components that were used to create the executable code. You must keep copies of the source and executable code and all data and configuration files. You should also record the versions of the operating system, libraries, **compilers** and other tools used to build the software. These may be required to build exactly the same system at some later date. This may mean that you have to store copies of the **platform** software and the tools used to create the system in the version management system along with the source code of the target system.

(571 Words)

III. Words to Note

executable	a.	可执行的
configuration	n.	配置
publicity	n.	宣传
scenario	n.	情景,局面
skip	v.	跳过,略过
upgrade	v.	提高,升级
infrequent	a.	罕见
alternative	a.	替代的
divergence	n.	分歧,背离
customized	a.	定制的
embedded	a.	嵌入的,植入的
compilers	n.	编译器
platform	n.	平台

IV. Text Understanding

Give brief answers to the following questions.

1) Do customers always install new systems? Why or why not?

2) Why can't new releases of the system rely on the installation of previous release?

3) What influence will the frequency of a system release have on mass-market software products?

4) Why is a custom software different from a mass market software?

5) How important it is to document a release? What should be documented?

V. Vocabulary Building

A. *Use words and expressions from the text to replace the underlined words and expressions. The first letter has been given.*

1) The relief agency will d _____ the food among several countries. (*Paragraph 1*)

2) If you want to e _____ that you catch the plane, take a taxi. (*Paragraph 1*)

3) You a _____ his innocence before hearing the evidence against him. (*Paragraph 2*)

4) That's just one hypothetical s _____. (*Paragraph 2*)

5) Should you write in _____ but long posts, or frequent but pithy ones, or something in between? (*Paragraph 4*)

6) We are very sad to have to do this, but there is no other a _____. (*Paragraph 4*)

7) They created a user-friendly platform that could be c _____ by organizations that wanted to advertise job opportunities online under their own brand. (*Paragraph 5*)

8) A shell splinter e _____ itself in the wall. (*Paragraph 5*)

9) The chemical c _____ obtained from roasting coffee beans at high temperatures were analyzed and quantified. (*Paragraph 6*)

10) We need to concentrate on our t _____ audience, namely women aged between 20 and 30. (*Paragraph 6*)

B. *Complete sentence with the words given.*

publicity	upgrade	scenario	configuration
alternative	executable	embedded	customized

1) The final section iterates the files in the directory to test whether they're _____.

2) Maybe you need to _____ your skills.

3) Skin cancers have also gotten significant _____.

4) This is a lose-lose _____.

5) We were researching to find _____ possibilities.

6) All fuel cells have the same basic _____; an electrolyte and two electrodes.

7) The next large-scale computing frontier will be about wearable devices and _____ computing.

8) But they still just put a discount on the shelf rather than give you a _____ one.

C. *Translate the following paragraph into Chinese.*

Preparing and distributing a system release is an expensive process, particularly for mass-market software products. If releases are too frequent, customers may not upgrade to the new release, especially when it is not free. If system releases are infrequent, market share may be lost as customers move to alternative systems. This, of course, does not apply to custom software developed specially for an organization. For custom software, infrequent releases may mean increasing divergence between the software and the business processes that it is designed to support.

Ⅵ. Further Reading

Software Release Life Cycle

A software release life cycle is the sum of the stages of development and maturity for a piece of computer software: ranging from its initial development to its eventual release, and including updated versions of the released version to help improve software or fix bugs still present in the software.

Usage of the "alpha/beta" test terminology originated at IBM. As long ago as the 1950s (and probably earlier), IBM used similar terminology for their hardware development. "A" test was the verification of a new product before public announcement. "B" test was the verification before releasing the product to be manufactured. "C" test was the final test before general availability of the product. As software became a significant part of IBM's offerings, the alpha test terminology was used to denote the pre-announcement test and beta test was used to show product readiness for general availability. Martin Belsky, a manager on some of IBM's earlier software projects claimed to have invented the terminology. IBM dropped the alpha/beta terminology during the 1960s, but by then it had received fairly wide notice. The usage of "beta test" which refers to testing done by customers was not done in IBM. Rather, IBM used the term "field test."

1. Pre-alpha

Pre-alpha refers to all activities performed during the software project before testing. These activities can include requirements analysis, software design, software development, and unit testing. In typical open source development, there are several types of pre-alpha versions. Milestone versions include specific sets of functions and are released as soon as the functionality is complete.

2. Alpha

The alpha phase of the release life cycle is the first phase to begin software testing (alpha is the first letter of the Greek alphabet, used as the number 1). In this phase, developers generally test the software using white box techniques. Additional validation is then performed using black box or gray box techniques, by another testing team. Moving to black box testing inside the organization is known as alpha release.

Alpha software can be unstable and could cause crashes or data loss. External availability of alpha software is uncommon in proprietary software. However, open source software, in particular, often have publicly available alpha versions, often distributed as the raw source code of the software. The alpha phase usually ends with a feature freeze, indicating that no more features will be added to the software. At this time, the software is said to be feature complete.

3. Beta

Beta, named after the second letter of the Greek alphabet, is the software development phase following alpha. It generally begins when the software is feature complete. Software in the beta phase will generally have many more bugs in it than complete software, as well as speed/performance issues and may still cause crashes or data loss. The focus of beta testing is reducing impacts to users, often incorporating usability testing. The process of delivering a beta version to the users is called beta release and this is typically the first time that the software is available outside of the organization that developed it.

The users of a beta version are called beta testers. They are usually customers or prospective customers of the organization that develops the software, willing to test the software without charge, often receiving the final software free of charge or for a reduced price. Beta version software is often useful for demonstrations and previews within an organization and to prospective customers. Some developers refer to this stage as a preview, prototype, technical preview (TP), or early access. Some software is kept in perpetual beta—where new features and functionality are continually added to the software without establishing a firm "final" release.

4. Open and closed beta

Developers release either a closed beta or an open beta. Closed beta versions are released to a restricted group of individuals for a user test by invitation, while open beta testers are from a larger group, or anyone interested. The testers report any bugs that they find, and sometimes suggest additional features they think should be available in the final version.

(673 Words)

A. *Explain the following terms briefly in your own words.*

| Pre-alpha | Alpha | Field test | Beta | Open and closed beta |

B. *Answer the questions below according to your understanding of the text.*

1) What are "A", "B", and "C" test respectively?

2) What are the disadvantages of alpha software?

3) What is "feature complete"?

4) What problems may beta phase have?

5) Which phase is the first time that the software is available outside?

6) Who are "beta testers"?

7) Why do developers refer to beta phase as a preview, prototype, technical preview (TP), or early access?

8) What is "perpetual beta"?

9) What are "open" and "closed" beta?

10) What is a "final version"?

C. *Match the words with their synonyms.*

maturity	a.	ripeness, adultness
initial	b.	premier, original
originated	c.	happen, occur
verification	d.	confirmation, validation
unstable	e.	mobile, variable

crashes	f.	fail, stop operating
proprietary	g.	privately owned and controlled
incorporating	h.	contain comprise

Cultural Notes

The term release candidate refers to a version with potential to be a final product, ready to release unless fatal bugs emerge. In this stage, the product features all designed functionalities and no known showstopper class bugs. At this phase the product is usually code completed.

Microsoft Corporation often uses the term release candidate. During the 1990s, Apple Computer used the term "golden master" for its release candidates, and the final golden master was the general availability release. Other terms include gamma (and occasionally also delta, and perhaps even more Greek letters) for versions that are substantially complete, but still under test, and omega for final testing of versions that are believed to be bug-free, and may go into production at any time. (Gamma, delta, and omega are, respectively, the third, fourth, and last letters of the Greek alphabet.) Some users disparagingly refer to release candidates and even final "point oh" releases as "gamma test" software, suggesting that the developer has chosen to use its customers to test software that is not truly ready for general release. Often, beta testers, if privately selected, will be billed for using the release candidate as though it were a finished product. A release is called code complete when the development team agrees that no entirely new source code will be added to this release. There may still be source code changes to fix defects. There may still be changes to documentation and data files, and to the code for test cases or utilities. New code may be added in a future release.

Part Two Writing

Writing Skills: Status Report

Creating a weekly status report of your work on a software project is vitally important to the success of the project. But it need not be drudgery, it can be exciting and rewarding.

I. Introduction

Most employees and contractors who work on software projects are required to file status reports. Regular status reports can make the difference between the success or failure of a software project. Since managers cannot gauge the progress of a software project just by oberservation alone, they depend on regular feedback from software builders like programmers, system analysts, instructional or game designers, technical writers and graphic artists to know if a project is going well, and if not, why.

II. What is a Status Report

Basically, staff members file status reports to inform supervisors and managers about the progress of ongoing software projects. Since status reporting is not an exact science, the required information varies with the company and even with the manager, but most status reports include some or all of the followings:

- Project start and completion dates.
- Which milestones you've passed.
- Percentage of the project that is complete.
- Any accomplishments worth mentioning.
- Important meetings attended.
- Any threats or potential risks to the projected timeline.
- Description of any problems you've encountered and resolved.
- Personnel or equipment limitations.

A status report is not just a copy of your daily activities for the past week. Status reports describe the work you've completed and forecasts how close you are to finish the project. Ultimately, these reports indicate whether your work is on schedule and if anything threatens you meeting the deadline.

III. What should the status report look like

Because status reports vary in format, length and delivery, it is difficult to nail down what to include in them. This is due to the communication format preferred by managers, which is dependent upon individual preferences. Some companies require verbal status reports every week. These verbal reports may be given in a group or one-on-one. Generally the staff member knows in advance the type of questions that will be asked or the format their group delivery should follow. While the verbal report is given, the manager writes down the salient points. Some employees like delivering verbal reports because it saves the time it would take to wite one themselves.

Most status reports, however, are submitted in written form and follow a preferred company format. All software projects have deadlines, and contain milestones throughout the project. Milestones make reporting and gauging progress much easier. If the project timeline does not contain milestones, then the status report should have a place to enter the percentage of the project you have completed.

IV. How Managers Use Status Reports

Project stakeholders want to know if the software project is going to be completed on time and within budget. Team managers, project managers and department heads combine their employee status reports into a broader report that is submitted to their next-level managers. This upper-level manager then forwards the essence of these reports to the stakeholders. On every level, status and progress reports depend on the information gathered from other managment levels, a process resembling dominos. For instance, if a project manager needs status reports from 10 people working on a project, but only receives 8, the report prepared will not be complete, nor will the ensuing reports.

V. How You Can Use Status Reports

Creating and filing a status report doesn't have to be painful. Actually, periodic status reports give you, the creative person, a chance to shine. If you work on a software project you probably spend hours and days alone, working on the computer. Creating a positive, upbeat status report gives you an opportunity to show how good you are and what you have done. If you have solved a problem, helped a coworker, posted a procedure, or passed a milestone, be sure to put it in your status report. It's like writing a little bio of yourself and the work you've done. Status report creating a weekly status report of your work on a software project is vitally important to the success of the project. But it needs not to be drudgery, it can be exciting and rewarding.

VI. Sample Writing

From: David Wallace Croft
To: Client or Project Manager
Subject: status report, David Croft, 2001-06-17

Weekly Status Report of
David Wallace Croft
for the Last Week Ending
2001-06-17 Sunday

A. Activities Planned for Last Week
- Document the revised architecture.
- Rework the database connectivity.
- Revise the installation documentation.

B. Activities Accomplished Last Week

- Discovered that source code files had been corrupted during project version control synchronization. In attempting to restore from backup, I was informed by the Sys Admin that the most recent run of the automatic backup process had already overwritten all files with the corrupted versions. I was further surprised to learn that periodic full backup snapshots are not created and stored off-site. Restored files to near original state by writing script to seek and remove all spurious characters.
- Implemented temporary backup solution.
- Documented the revised architecture.

C. Activities Planned for Next Week

- Track progress of systems backup policy revision request.
- Rework the database connectivity.
- Revise the installation documentation.

D. New Issues

We need to create full backups periodically and store them off-site.

E. Old Issues

The application server needs to be upgraded.

David Wallace Croft, Senior Software Architect
CroftSoft, Inc. (http://www.croftsoft.com/)
(214) 731-9284 / david@croftsoft.com

VII. Seven Steps for writing a status report

- **Subject Line**

Assuming that the status reports will be sent by email and then archived in message folders sortable by subject, using a consistent subject line format can make searching for a particular status report much easier.

- **Activities Planned for Last Week**

This will always be a cut-and-paste verbatim copy of the content of the "Activities Planned for Next Week" section from the previous status report. Although redundant, this allows the report reviewer to quickly compare the activities projected with the activities actually accomplished as documented in the immediately following section.

The report author will use this section to remind himself of planned activities as he fills in the template with his accomplishments throughout the week. Many developers print a paper copy of this section and pin it to their wall at the beginning of each new reporting period for quick reference. This promotes a concentration of focus and a sense of progress as each planned activity on the list is initiated and completed.

- **Activities Accomplished Last Week**

This section is the heart of the report. The accurate documentation of recent activities facilitates management by the employer and communicates progress to the client. It provides the employee with the opportunity to advertise his contributions and permits the contractor to justify his invoice.

The activities actually accomplished in the previous week may or may not have any relationship to what was planned. It is important to both the author and the reviewer that actual activities are listed, regardless of whether planned or not, in order to validate and manage the consumption of time and labor.

Throughout the week the report author will add items to this section as they are accomplished. This incremental approach ensures that all relevant activities are recorded and reduces the probability that a report will be delayed or skipped due to the difficulty of writing the report when memories have faded or the deadline is imminent.

It is recommended that the author avoid delaying the submission of a report for the purpose of including additional activities within this section. Likewise, it is not necessary to delay "closing" this section until full and complete accomplishment of a subtask. The intent of periodic reports is to act as a regular and consistent snapshot in time of actual progress. Furthermore, intentional delays by the author may have the unintended effect of increasing developer stress as the report itself then becomes yet another overdue task. By establishing a consistent pattern of punctual report delivery, an author can increase reviewer confidence.

- **Activities Planned for Next Week**

In this section, the report author records what he anticipates his activities will be for the coming week. Note that we use the phrases "Last Week" and "Next Week" instead of "This Week" to prevent ambiguity. The report is assumed to be written just after the end of all activity for "Last Week" and just before any activity is initiated for "Next Week".

These planned activities should vary from week to week in sufficient details that a reviewer can detect the rate of progress. For example, a very general planned activity such as "Work on user interface" can be uninformative if simply repeated week after week without breaking it down into subtasks.

This section has the effect of promoting the temporary cessation of activity for a moment of reflection and review. By requiring the report author to update this section on a weekly basis with relevant content, the exercise will lead to a reevaluation of short-term goals in light of the current project status and external forces.

An additional beneficial effect of this section is that it prevents misunderstanding and miscommunication between the developer and the project manager or client. In reviewing the planned activities for the next week as documented by the developer within the role of report author, the reviewer has the opportunity to clarify any misinterpretations of expectations and redirect short-term goals if necessary.

- **New Issues**

The new issues section is a place for the author to alert the reviewer to any current or projected problems that may delay or derail the scheduled delivery. It may be as simple as a planned vacation or as complicated as blocked task requiring management attention.

- **Old Issues**

This section is a weekly reminder to the reviewer of problem issues that have been previously reported by not yet been resolved. This low-priority reminder is always placed at the bottom of the report as it may become quite lengthy over time with only minor updates from week to week.

As the content for this section may not frequently change, it is likely that regular reviewers will skim past this section. For this reason, any new issue should not be placed within the Old Issues section until they have been introduced within the New Issues section in the current or a previous report. Furthermore, such issues should be copied verbatim from the New Issues to the Old Issues section as any rewording may contribute new information which may never be read or require the unnecessary reexamination of an issue previously described in other terms.

- **Contact Information**

A status report reviewer will frequently desire to contact the author for further explanation on one or more of the included topics. Providing contact information within the closing signature block obviates the need for the readers to retrieve that information from his records, which may or may not be readily available, on a periodic basis over an extended period of time. It is especially useful to include a phone number as the reader may not have access to a network connection at the time of review.

VIII. Exercise

What are the functions of each part in writing status report? Choose a ~ j from Box 2 to match the seven sections in Box 1. You may choose more than one for each section.

1. BOX 1

Subject Line Activities Planned for Last Week Activities Accomplished Last Week Activities Planned for Next Week New Issues Old Issues Contact Information	

2. BOX 2

a.	Promoting the temporary cessation of activity for a moment of reflection and review.
b.	Include a phone number.
c.	Alert the reviewer to any current or projected problems that may delay or derail the scheduled delivery.
d.	Prevents misunderstanding and miscommunication between the developer and the project manager or client.
e.	Increase reviewer confidence.
f.	Using a consistent format.
g.	Detect the rate of progress.
h.	The heart of the report.
i.	A weekly reminder of problem issues that have been previously reported by not yet been resolved.
j.	Promotes a concentration of focus and a sense of progress as each planned activity.

Part Three Case Study

Why You Shouldn't Expect Too Much From Apple's Next iPhone Software Release

Last November, Apple changed its executive leadership when it ousted Scott Forstall, who led development of the iPhone from its inception.

A lot of people saw the management shakeup as a sign that Apple was preparing for a major overhaul of iOS, the software that powers iPhones, iPads, and iPod Touches.

An iOS overhaul could be in the works, but if people are expecting it this year, they're probably going to be let down.

Forstall's role was split between two people: Jony Ive, who would oversee the look and feel of Apple's mobile software, iOS, and Craig Federighi, who would lead the other aspects of the software.

With Forstall out, a lot of people started excitedly speculating about how iOS would change. One of the biggest complaints about Apple's software from the tech press was that it was larded with excessively detailed graphics.

Steve Jobs preferred making apps that looked like their real life counterpart. For instance, the notes app looks like a legal pad, completed with fake ripped sheets at the top. After Jobs died, Forstall continued this legacy in apps like Podcasts which had a fake tape machine running in the background.

Crisp lines and minimalism define Ive's hardware design. The assumption is that Ive will bring that same vision for clean design to iOS and wipe out some of the gaudy excess of Forstall.

This could happen, but if Ive is going to change iOS, it's going to take time. Apple can't rejigger iOS in six months.

Speaking on John Gruber's podcast last week, Guy English, an iOS developer who was friendly with people at Apple said that he knew iOS 7 wasn't going to be radically different. He warned that it wasn't based on inside information, but rather years of experience in product development.

"Just the way product planning works and time lines, there's no way they're rebooting all of iOS 7 after Forstall left," he said. "Maybe iOS 8 will be interesting, but iOS 7 will be less of a leap than many people are hoping for."

Gruber, one the smartest bloggers on Apple, said the same thing: "A lot of people expect iOS 7 to be new, new, new, and they're going to be disappointed, disappointed, disappointed." If Apple has ideas for changing iOS significantly, look for them in 2014.

I. Team Activity

Read the codes and commentary below. Discuss in a group:

1) Check in the Internet and find out how often does Apple update its iOS?
2) What do you think about Apple's iOS system? Which one is the most significant?
3) What do you think about iOS 7?

II. Assignment

Use specific examples to illustrate a software release life cycle.

References

[1] Outsourcing—What is Outsourcing. http://www.sourcingmag.com/content/what_is_outsourcing.asp, 2014-7-16.

[2] Ron Babin, Brian Nicholson. Sustainable Global Outsourcing. Palgrave Macmillan, 2013.

[3] Helen Coster (May 3, 2010). Ten Tips for Better Business Writing. http://www.forbes.com/2010/05/03/better-business-writing-leadership-careers-tips.html, 2014-7-16.

[4] Merill Mathews (July 20, 2012). Companies 'Outsource' Because That's Where The Sales Are. http://www.forbes.com/sites/merrillmatthews/2012/07/20/companies-outsource-because-thats-where-the-sales-are, 2014.

[5] Stormy Friday (February, 2005). Avoiding Culture Clash When Selecting Providers of Outsourced Services. http://www.facilitiesnet.com/facilitiesmanagement/article/Outlook--2569#.

[6] Sunit Jilla (November 30, 1999). Managing Culture When Outsourcing. http://www.outsourcemagazine.co.uk.

[7] Learning the Corporate Culture. http://spot.pcc.edu/~rjacobs/career/learning_the_corporate_culture.htm.

[8] Stages of the Writing Process. http://wenku.baidu.com/link?url = oyXBhGooq6Zlg _ m _ o08zIokWEqsU _ oUdRaK-5YrB4XIItpSfI52J _ f-q8JRyfqM9CRCvVUBs9BvZyCykkMr _ pwfsO5jstauI2-mpruK7RKQS.

[9] The Chinese-German Team. http://buinternationalmanagement.wikispaces.com/file/view/German + v + Chinese. + How + they + view + each + other.docx.

[10] Keys To Successful Outsourcing: How To Make Your Clients Happy". http://blog.socketsandlightbulbs.com/2013/03/24/keys-to-successful-outsourcing-how-to-make-your-clients-happy, 2014.

[11] Brent Galloway (2013). Four brilliant ways to handle client changes you don't want to make. http://www.graphicdesignblender.com/four-brilliant-ways-to-handle-client-changes-you-dont-want-to-make # comments, 2014.

[12] Template of Complaint Letter. Consumer Action Handbook (2001). Federal consumer Information Center, Pueblo, CO, 82009. www.pueblo.gsa.gov, 2014.

[13] Thomas Muller (May 12, 2012). Internet Service Provider Issues: A Case Study. http://www.complaintexpert.co.uk/internet-service-provider-case-study.html, 2014.

[14] Susan M Heathfield. "How to Build a Teamwork Culture". http://humanresources.about.com/od/involvementteams/a/team_culture.htm, 2014.

[15] Susan M Heathfield. 12 Tips for Team Building—How to Build Successful Work Teams. http://humanresources.about.com/od/involvementteams/a/twelve_tip_team.htm, 2014.

[16] How to Write Memos. http://www2.elc.polyu.edu.hk/cill/eiw/memos.htm, 2014.

[17] Janet M. Six (May 23, 2011). Teamwork and Collaboration Across Departments. http://www.uxmatters.com/mt/archives/2011/05/teamwork-and-collaboration-across-departments.php, 2014.

[18] How to write a Project Initiation Document. http://www.bizbodz.com/Management/Project-Management/How-to-write-a-Project-Initiation-Document-1.asp, 2014.

[19] William D Engelke. Writing an Outsourcing Contract. http://www.hsv.com/writers/engel/outsou3.html, 2014.

[20] How to Write Business Contract. http://www.wikihow.com/Write-a-Business-Contract, 2014.

[21] Project Initiation Documents-Getting Your Project Off to a Great Start. http://www.mindtools.com/pages/article/newPPM_85.htm, 2014.

[22] Tom Mochal. Defining Project Goals and Objectives. http://www.kidasa.com/information/articles/goals, 2014.

[23] Engineering Design Process. http://en.wikipedia.org/wiki/Engineering_design_process, 2014.

[24] How to Write E-mail. http://elc.polyu.edu.hk/cill/eiw/e-mail.aspx, 2014.

[25] 10 Tips to Ensure the Success of Your Design Projects. http://vandelaydesign.com/successful-design-projects/, 2014.

[26] Common Coding Language. http://www.codeconquest.com/what-is-coding/common-programming-languages/.

[27] Coding Techniques and Programming Practices. http://www.codeconquest.com/what-is-coding/how-does-coding-work/.

[28] Meeting Minutes Format. http://www.buzzle.com/articles/meeting-minutes-format.html.

[29] Coding Techniques and Programming Practices. http://msdn.microsoft.com/en-us/library/aa260844(v=vs.60).aspx.

[30] Douglas Thomas. Hacker Culture. books.google.com.hk/books?isbn=1452904286.

[31] Introduction to Coding Guidelines for Cocoa. https://developer.apple.com/library/prerelease/mac/documentation/Cocoa/Conceptual/CodingGuidelines/CodingGuidelines.html.

[32] Software release life cycle. http://en.wikipedia.org/wiki/Software_release_life_cycle.

[33] Software Release Life Cycle. http://www.cybermetrics.com/GAGEtrak7/software_lifecycle.htm.

[34] Ann Gordon. (December 31, 2012). Creating Status Reports for Software Projects: The Fundamentals. http://www.brighthubpm.com/templates-forms/2068-creating-status-reports-for-software-projects-part-one/.

[35] Jay Yarow Mar (2013). Why You Shouldn't Expect Too Much From Apple's Next iPhone Software Release. http://www.businessinsider.com/apples-ios-7-wont-be-a-major-overhaul-2013-3#ixzz37h7aSvID.

[36] David Lile Brown. The Five Essentials For Software Testing. http://www.isixsigma.com/industries/software-it/five-essentials-software-testing/.

[37] What Does a Software Test Engineer Do. http://www.wisegeek.com/what-does-a-software-test-engineer-do.htm.

[38] Nicholas Katers. How Does a Software Tester Spend a Workday. http://www.ehow.com/how-does_4701697_software-tester-spend-workday.html.

[39] Software testing. http://en.wikipedia.org/wiki/Software_testing.

[40] How to Write Effective Emails to QA (or any) Team. http://www.softwaretestinghelp.com/how-to-write-effective-emails-to-qa-team/.

[41] TechWell Contributor. Managing the Testing Process. http://www.stickyminds.com/article/managing-testing-process.

[42] Ian Sommerville. Software Engineering. China Machine Press, 2006.

[43] Keys To Successful Outsourcing: How To Make Your Clients Happy (March 24, 2013). http://blog.socketsandlightbulbs.com/2013/03/24/keys-to-successful-outsourcing-how-to-make-your-clients-happy/,

2014-4-10.

[44] Brent Galloway (2013). Four brilliant ways to handle client changes you don't want to make. http://www.graphicdesignblender.com/four-brilliant-ways-to-handle-client-changes-you-dont-want-to-make#comments, 2014-4-10.

[45] Template of Complaint Letter. Consumer Action Handbook (2001). Federal consumer Information Center, Pueblo, CO, 82009. www.pueblo.gsa.gov, 2014-4-10.

[46] Thomas Muller (May 12, 2012). Internet Service Provider Issues: A Case Study. http://www.complaintexpert.co.uk/internet-service-provider-case-study.html, 2014-4-10.

[47] Dr David M Anderson, P E, CMC (August, 2011). Outsourcing; The Reality For Cost Reduction. http://www.halfcostproducts.com/outsourcing.htm, 2014-4-18.

[48] Norman Grossman (January 24, 2012). Creating Sustainable Cost Management Through Outsourcing. PRNewswire. http://www.prnewswire.com/news-releases/creating-sustainable-cost-management-through-outsourcing-137943113.html, 2014-4-18.

[49] Enterprise Solutions Introduction. http://www.comptechdoc.org/independent/enterprise/, 2014-4-18.

[50] David G Meeker, Jay P Mortensen (2011). Outsourcing to China, A Case Study Revisited Seven Years Later. http://www.dfma.com/truecost/revisited.pdf, 2014-4-18.

[51] Quality Assurance for Outsourcing Software Development Project (April 3, 2013). HKSTCC. http://hkstcc.org/en/publications_detail.php?c=quality-assruance-for-outsourcing-software-development-project, 2014-6-26.

[52] Michael Cobb. Outsourcing security issues: Managing outsourced software development. http://www.computerweekly.com/tip/Outsourcing-security-issues-Managing-outsourced-software-development, 2014-6-26.

[53] Randall S Hansen, Ph D. Step-by-Step Guide to Researching Companies: How to Conduct Job-Search Research. http://www.quintcareers.com/researching_companies_guide.html, 2014-6-26.

[54] Louis Columbus (March 18, 2014). The Best Enterprise Software Companies And CEOs To Work For In 2014. Forbes. http://www.forbes.com/sites/louiscolumbus/2014/03/18/the-best-enterprise-software-companies-and-ceos-to-work-for-in-2014/, 2014-6-26.

[55] Darren Dahl (January 1, 2006). Case Study: Was Outsourcing to India the Right Move. http://www.inc.com/magazine/20060101/handson-casestudy.html#ixzz36NSeLsEC, 2014-6-26.

[56] Joe McKendrick (October 23, 2012). Cloud is Disrupting the Outsourcing Industry. Forbes. http://www.forbes.com/sites/joemckendrick/2012/10/23/cloud-is-disrupting-the-outsourcing-industry/, 2014-7-1.

[57] The Future of Outsourcing in India. http://www.outsource2india.com/trends/future_outsourcing.asp, 2014-7-1.

[58] Cloud computing. http://en.wikipedia.org/wiki/Cloud_computing, 2014-7-1.

[59] 3 Examples of Cloud Success. http://www.outsystems.com/offer/ebook/3-examples-of-cloud-success/?utm_source=MSN&utm_medium=CPC&utm_term=cloud%20success&utm_content=cloud%20success&utm_campaign=SEARCH%20-%20UK%20-%20eBooks, 2014-7-1.